OFF THE GRID
AND OVER THE HILL

Lynne Farr

CREATESPACE.COM

Cover design by Patti Millington

Back cover photo: Shingo Honda

Eve Luckring's poem on page 18 was first published
in the journal *Ribbons* Vol 2: #2: 2006

ISBN: 978-1-4662-0937-4

Library of Congress Control Number: 2011915140

Printed in the United States of America.

Preface

Off The Grid And Over The Hill is a sequel to the book *Off The Grid Without A Paddle*. It continues the true story of two greenhorns, husband and wife, who ditched downtown Los Angeles for the great unknown: country life, off the grid, in a mountain rainforest in rural Hawaii.

By now, they've spent over five years without the wonders of modern existence: there's no automatic electricity, no city water, natural gas is not piped in. There's no sewer system, no garbage pickup, no phone line, no street maintenance, no street address, and no postal delivery.

Solar panels light a lightbulb, water comes from the sky, heat is from woodstoves, phone calls bounce off a satellite, and all the other missing city services require them to do-it-yourself.

She thought a DIY lifestyle would keep them young, but old age looms like that blue-gray Hawaiian rain cloud thumbing its nose on the horizon. He still chops down trees for firewood but then has to go lie down for a while. She can't carry a full five gallon gas can to the generator any more. He can but he doesn't want to.

This book asks: How old do you have to be before living off the grid becomes a pain in your Paradise?

More urgently: How old is OLD?

For the answers to these and other important questions of survival, read on . . .

i

Contents

CONTENTS Continued

"I'm so old they've cancelled my blood type."
– Bob Hope

"When I was a boy the Dead Sea was only sick."
– George Burns

"He's so old that when he orders a three-minute egg, they ask for the money up front."
– Milton Berle

"I'm sixty five and I guess that puts me in with the geriatrics, but if there were fifteen months in every year, I'd only be forty-eight."
– James Thurber

"If I'd known I was going to live this long, I'd have taken better care of myself."
– Eubie Blake

1

WE'RE STILL HERE

Remember the old joke about The Lone Ranger and his side-kick Tonto as five thousand Apaches with weapons and war-paint appear, whooping, on the horizon?

"Tonto, we'd better get outta here!" implores The Lone Ranger.

Says Tonto, "Who's WE white man?"

The "WE" in the title of this chapter are your devoted author Lynne Farr and my husband, Japanese painter, printmaker, and installation artist, Shingo (say it like "Bingo") Honda.

Previously dyed-in-the-wool city-types, we did "get outta here." Way "outta here."

In 2005 we moved from downtown Los Angeles to the East side of the Big Island of Hawaii, to a handbuilt wooden home on half an acre of land, at the end of an almost uninhabited country lane, half a mile from the nearest paved road, in a mountain rainforest.

There's no electric grid, no county water, no natural gas, no sewer system, no phone line, no TV reception, no street address, no postal delivery, no garbage pickup, and no road maintenance.

What were we thinking?

Why would we buy a place that's so un-First World?

Why would we move to a house that's so remote, that spends its days and nights making lists of chores for us to do?

1

Didn't we realize we were the ones who'd have to haul propane for the stove, fridge, and on-demand hot water heater? Haul garbage to the dump? Cut wood for the woodstoves? Drive five miles to get the mail? Haul gravel for the road?

And those are just the basics. Weren't we paying attention?

We were used to living in the lofts of L. A.'s Artists' District. If we needed services we called the landlord (who might or might not provide them). We'd never been home-owners together. We'd never even lived together in a house.

But our escapade, a last fling, having been flung, has turned out to be a first-class adventure. Well, perhaps "premium-economy with special meals" might be a better description.

For economy there's the fact that an off-grid house was cheaper to buy and should be cheaper to run: "cheaper" is a word that's close to my heart.

For the premium, there's the rainforest. Picture a world of green-on-green as a backdrop for eye-popping color; lacy fern-trees with ever-blooming Valentines, the heart-shaped red and orange and pink anthurium flowers growing under them, and a cheerful bouquet of orchids and bromeliads growing on them. It's a botanical bonanza outside our windows.

We've almost forgotten that we moved here in the 100 year record rains, with downpours so long and so loud that we missed our smoggy but not soggy Southern California former home. That months-long deluge, once it was behind us, made us permanently grateful for the somewhat sunnier days ahead.

Then, there's the almost uninhabited aspect of things: it's so quiet here, it's private, something unheard of in Downtown L.A., though more people are moving into the area and we occasionally hear the sounds of bulldozers and chainsaws beating up on trees.

The almost uninhabited country lane is also unpaved and usually full of potholes, but this means we're blessed with a relatively traffic-free environment: who wants to jolt down a bumpy, muddy, one-lane road that leads to nowhere? We might not hear a car for days. Which tends to make us jump a little higher when pig hunters start shooting.

But at least no bullets come through the windows as they used to during the gang wars we endured in L. A. – one neighbor had her young son sleeping in the bathtub for protection.

More gunshots means fewer pigs, or so it seems. We haven't seen a wild pig in a year: no meandering pig families with dear little piglets trailing their Moms. No enormous boars with tusks peering out of the woods and scaring the daylights out of us.

No pigs means less excitement but more vegetables in the garden. And more pineapples. And more bananas. (Special meals.)

And no giant muddy gouges out of the front lawn. And no disappearing heliconia and anthurium plants, yanked out by their roots. These days there's no shortage of anything a feral pig has the munchies for. As Martha Stewart might say, "No pigs: it's a good thing."

A pair of pheasants do come to call, and we often hear roosters crowing in the distance. But there are none close by. That's another good thing: no ear-splitting wake-up calls.

The fact that electric lines only come halfway down the road, and that it would cost at least twenty-five thousand dollars to bring them to our house, means that we will never, ever, have to look at electric poles and overhead wires.

No phone lines either: we rely on cell phones for our contact with the outside world.

Solar panels and the sun provide electricity, as long as there *is* some sun here in the, uh, rainforest. But if not, we have our adorable Honda generator.

You may think it odd to describe a piece of electrical equipment as "adorable" but the generator is. It's good-looking with its bright red paint and smart black trim. It's easy to operate with its key-start and smooth choke. It's quiet, so we can run it early or late without annoying racket. It's frugal on gas. On the rainiest of rainy days (or weeks) when we don't get enough voltage from the sun, running the generator for about an hour gives us power for the rice cooker, or the toaster; keeps the lights on, and the Netflix movies playing via the DVD player.

The generator's more like the family pet than a tool, so we feed it well with fuel that's free of ethanol and give it treats of a new spark plug and carburetor cleaner.

We've come a long technological way from our first days here when we unwittingly bought a house with only two solar panels, four batteries, and a noisy Neanderthal generator.

Looking back, I can't believe my long-suffering husband had to hook up a battery charger from the generator to the batteries every night, in all weathers, mostly rain. "Don't get a shock!"

Nobody said he shouldn't have to. And we never questioned it. We were such off-grid no-nothings, newbies, nitwits – pick one.

Without going too far out on a limb, I'd say we're doing much better now, though we just spent two days of a long weekend without running water when our pump broke down, and the back-up didn't work, and the store where you buy them was closed, and our favorite handyman, who knows how to fix them, was out of town for the holiday.

The bucket brigade from our outdoor water tank to the kitchen and bathrooms reminded me that many women in this world carry water long distances every day from muddy puddles, so different from our clean and plentiful, nearby supply. What was also different was that my husband helped carry the buckets.

Shingo Honda is a great off-grid partner, though he always disputes my use of the word "great."

"Einstein great. Picasso great," he admonishes. "Other people, you need find different word," he insists, using his own brand of English which we call "Shinglish."

But never mind what he says, I still say he's great. Despite his original reluctance to leave friends and all that was familiar behind in Los Angeles, he's adapted completely to our off-grid life, with none of the easy amenities of the city.

He takes care of our water supply, climbing on the roof to clean debris out of the gutters, a must, because, for flushing, bathing and dishwashing, water comes from the sky, slides off the roof into the gutters, and is collected in a small above-ground swimming pool known as a "catchment." When the pump, which gives us running water, breaks, he replaces it, with a minimum of swearing when the replacement doesn't work and we have to wait for Michael MacMillan, a Phd. in pump, to come back from his well deserved weekend vacation and bail us out of yet another off-grid scrape.

Shingo changes the water filters and maintains the on-demand hot-water heater. He installed a new cover on the catchment which meant he had to spend a morning up to his armpits in 4,500 gallons of chilly water. "Don't pee!"

Once a month he hauls two propane tanks, 54 pounds when full, which fuel our refrigerator, stove, and water heater. He carries and hoists five gallon bottles of drinking water, times four. He takes a heavy load of sheets and towels and clothing to the laundry in Hilo. (We still don't have a washer/dryer: why is too complicated to explain.)

He does all this without stopping and he's romantic, too. More or less.

The other day I was making Mexican food, chicken tostadas, using dried black beans which have to boil forever. I forgot to set a timer and the water boiled away. Too late, I smelled the unmistakable aroma of cremated black beans and went running into the kitchen.

Shingo followed.

"I love you," he laughed, as I threw away both beans and pot.

"Why?" I said, feeling really stupid.

"Because you really stupid. You no perfect. Like me," he said, in his endearing ESL, as he gave me a hug.

His hug, quite un-Japanese, doesn't shrink from bodily contact. It envelops. It encompasses. It openly offers his amazing energy: energy I credit to naps.

He naps after lunch. He naps if he's bored. No day goes by without a nap.

Lately, though, he's been apologizing for naps and referring to our house as a retirement home.

He'll say, as he lapses into dreams, "Sorry. ⋅ I am old man," but I point out that he's been taking naps as long as I've known him, and

5

that would be more than twenty years. I don't go along with this "old man" business. I don't want it to be true.

Shingo Honda, not an old man, a fine artist who naps, painted the house.

He painted it the color of mold. Really.

The exterior was originally natural pine with a clear coating, but not long after we moved in, we noticed it was going moldy.

Every available anti-mold remedy was used to get rid of the greenish-brown streaks, and some of them lightened the color of the damage but nothing erased it, not even straight bleach.

Since mold thrives in damp conditions and we'd moved to what was already the rainy side of Hawaii Island in those non-stop 100 year rains, we couldn't exactly call customer service if a fungus-foiler didn't work, it was simply being handed an impossible assignment.

After talking to new friends on the island, and from observation, we realized that just painting the house wasn't necessarily going to solve the problem: light colored paints went moldy, too. So we settled on a dark olive/brown paint with the nicely descriptive name "Fedora." If you can picture Humphrey Bogart's hat, you'll be able to imagine the color we chose. If this paint goes moldy, believe me, nobody's going to know.

But here in our constantly rainy climate it's not so easy to get paint onto a house.

On a given day, Shingo would survey the sky, find it blue with fluffy white clouds, and decide to paint. He'd get his rollers and brushes ready and the ladder up, mix and pour the paint into his paint tray, climb the ladder and begin, when ("Oh, no!") rain. Repeat. Repeat – in East Hawaii, it's a question of sneaking through the raindrops.

Shingo, despite naps, is a man who likes to get it done. He likes to finish. He wants to see results, write "The End" to the project, and go on to the next.

But this paint job, we soon realized, would have to be a little-by-little, weather-permitting, kind of thing. Sure, the house would look strange with some surfaces painted, others not, and the end-date unknown, but "Shikatanai," we'd use his favorite Japanese expression, "Cannot be helped."

As the work progressed and blank spaces filled, I began to love the subtle hue we'd chosen. It's an industrial/architectural color but at the same time, almost traditional here in Hawaii where many people paint their homes in dark tones, maybe for the same reason we did. An unexpected bonus is that it melts the house right into the forest. Looking through the trees, you can hardly tell it's there.

After weeks of off-and-on, Shingo finished the job. And it looked spectacular. We went out to dinner to celebrate.

But the next morning, when we strolled outside to further admire his handiwork in full sunshine, we observed, with dismay, that the paint had begun to blister. Not everywhere, just on a few surfaces that were exposed to strong, hot, sun. But, wherever it was happening, the building looked diseased.

I consulted the paint department at Home Depot in Hilo where we bought the paint. Shingo consulted our knowledgeable friend Russell Nakao. The consensus was the same. "Bad prep."

"What primer did you use?" asked Russell, who had just successfully painted his own house.

"What meaning . . . primer?" said my husband.

"Primer" can mean more than one thing in English. It might mean a base coat of paint. It might mean the English text book he was supposed to study in school, but never did. Either way, the word didn't make it into his vocabulary.

Cut to: poor Shingo on a ladder dangerously perched on a piece of lumber spanning our tiny fishpond, scraping and sanding and priming and repainting one of the offending walls.

Cut to: The next day as he observed that one corner, which hadn't needed repainting, had suddenly broken out in new bubbles and blisters.

"Huh?!!!"

I know that sound of distress. Having put away all his painting gear, I knew he'd be dragging it out again immediately if something wasn't done.

"Alright, enough!" I told the perfectionist. "Stop! No one's ever going to notice a few bubbles in the paint. If I don't see it, nobody will," I cajoled. "So stop! Please go back to making art!"

Of course, I do see the remaining blisters. Some of them are more than an inch across. They look awful. It's like zooming in on poison oak. But, I'd rather live with a happy artist than an obsessed house painter any day.

Now, I have a question . . .

Have I dated myself by referring to The Lone Ranger and Tonto at the start of this chapter?

If you're not receiving Social Security, maybe you don't even know who The Lone Ranger is.

Let me clarify that he and Tonto, fictional frontier lawmen in the American West, defenders of the weak, righters of wrongs, and expert horsemen – the Masked Man rode "Silver" and Tonto rode "Scout" – were first seen in a comic strip in 1938, which is before I was born.

Though, as a kid, I did enjoy their adventures on radio, (clippity-clop, clippity-clop) which I used to listen to, curled up in front of my parents' mahogany console radio/record player, a piece of furniture which dominated their living room – this was before we or any of our neighbors had TV.

Oops! Now I've definitely dated myself.

Well, then . . . Shikatanai. Cannot be helped. Because age will be an essential part of this story. Put this book down right now if you're not up for it.

Age is going to weigh heavily on this tale of off-grid life and the decisions we make about how to live it. Face it, it's going to affect everything we do from here on in.

So maybe I'd better just get it over with right now, spit it out, drop the other shoe, spill the burnt beans:

How old am I?

Okay (deep breath) here goes . . .

At 70, I'm one year younger than The Lone Ranger.

Shingo? He's 66, like the Route.

Ahhhhh! That was cleansing!

8

Though 66, in my opinion, is far from old, there are telltale signs of Shingo's advancing age.

When we first moved here he filled our woodpile, cutting down dead trees in the forest with a chain saw, chopping them into wood-stove likely lengths, and then splitting the biggest logs with a long-handled axe raised over his head and brought down, karate fashion, with a scream: "Hyiaaa!" He could split a huge log in two with a single stroke.

But for the last couple of years we've been buying wood.

It started once we realized that wood from our land has to be seasoned, allowed to dry for at least a year and preferably two, for it to burn well.

Ironically, the man who chain-saws and splits and seasons the wood we buy, George Indie, is 77.

And so is his truck. At least it looks it: all rusted out and the truckbed replaced with plywood which is already worn through.

George used to carry a surfboard on the rack of his pick-up and go to the ocean almost daily, but he got hurt last year and decided to give up his lifetime passion. His new passion is gold, he tells us. He's saving up to go to California and go panning.

We've been spoiled by George Indie. Although we have a lot of two year old wood from our land, stacked and ready for use, and Shingo still chops down dead trees before they fall on us, and cuts them down to woodstove length with a chain-saw, he's not hurrying to hand-split the bigger logs.

Having been away from it for awhile, he may be concerned that he can't come up with the karate power of concentration or the strength to whack the biggest logs in half. Whatever the reason, there's a lack of "Hyiaaa!" in our back yard.

Shingo seems surprised by his age. He doesn't look 66. He's trim and fit and hasn't changed much physically in the years I've known him. He's shocked when his stamina isn't what it used to be or when other people assume he's weaker than he wants to be.

Perhaps influenced by George Indie who was still surfing at the time, Shingo decided, a couple of years ago, to take up boogie-boarding.

He started with small waves but couldn't wait to go out to the big break off Richardson's Beach in Hilo, where we could always see teens and young adults cavorting.

I like to snorkel there but never go far from shore, so Shingo usually invited a younger Japanese friend so they could keep an eye on each other.

After their first trip out they both commented that the break was much farther away than it looked. But before long, they began to catch some satisfying waves.

I could spot Shingo by the bright orange kerchief he wore to shield his bald-shaved head from the sun. (I'll just explain, here, that he shaves his head because, as well as being an artist, he's a Soto Zen Buddhist priest. But more about that later.)

One day we went to the beach and his chum couldn't come, so Shingo decided to go boogie-boarding on his own. I went for my usual snorkel around the reef and returned to the beach to wait for him. When he came back he wasn't saying much.

"So, how was it?" I asked.

After a pause, and a shake of the head, he blurted in his best Shinglish, "I so embarrassing!"

"Why? What happened?"

Apparently, after spending too much energy on the long swim out to the break, he was waiting for a wave. He must have looked pretty pooped, because a young surfer paddled up to him and gently said:

"Uncle, it's too big out here for you today. Would you like some help getting back to shore?"

The term "uncle" is such a sweet one here in Hawaii. It means we're all related, which of course we are. And it shows respect for elders. But Shingo didn't want to be the boy's uncle. He wanted to be his equal.

He realized the kindly kid was right, though, about the size of the wave and the danger of the day. Though he declined the young man's help, he paddled slowly back to the beach.

Since then he's been choosing to be gentler on himself, snorkling more than boogie-boarding. But in this case, I think his change in attitude has less to do with age and more to do with experience.

No matter how old you are, you lack experience in something.

We, both glaring greenhorns, had no experience of off-grid life or country life when we moved to Hawaii Island in 2005.

We still lack knowledge and understanding of many off-grid, hinterland, Hawaiian things.

But what we don't know, somebody does.

Somebody knows what they're doing.

Witness Shingo's "nephew" out in the ocean.

Witness George Indie, at his age, still splitting logs for a living.

And then there's Michael McMillan of Michael's Repair, who fixed our water pump, not just once but three times; repaired the stove, refrigerator, and leaking kitchen sink; supplied and installed a new, larger, on-demand hot water heater – Shingo can now have a blazing hot bath without boiling vats of water on the stove; talked us, by phone, through a reset of the solar system one Fourth of July, when we blew out the electricity with a houseful of guests, then wouldn't accept any payment; adjusted the charge-controller (don't ask me to describe what that is) so we use the generator less; put in four new solar panels, and replaced four batteries which died.

And how about electrical engineer Rich Reha, whom we barely knew, who volunteered to come to the house to teach us about the solar system? Then, realizing our inability to absorb even the rudiments of his tutorial – think non-mathematical woman and man who speaks cute but limited English – he offered to install a switch next to our bed so we can turn off the inverter (don't ask me what that is, either) last thing at night, thereby turning off all the electricity in the house and saving enough power to make toast in the morning. It's known around here as "Rich's Switch," but we think of it as Rich's magic secret.

And let's not forget the young library technician in Mountain View who advised me that the reason movies on DVD were flipping and flapping at our place, usually during the most important plot points, had nothing to do with an ebb in electricity. What we should do, and did, was to buy an inexpensive new DVD player because the newer ones have stronger lasers.

And (may he be inducted into to the High Tech Hall of Fame) there's the young man at Apple who spent over an hour on the phone with me re-programming my new cell-phone-as-modem wireless connection to the internet, when it unexpectedly failed. He walked me through terminology I never will understand, even allowing both of us to take a bathroom break, then called to finish up and get me back on line, though my free Apple Care minutes had run out.

It's because of these and countless other people, on and off this uniquely beautiful island, because of their experience and expertise, that we're still here. And I don't just mean here in Hawaii, or here off the grid, but here on Earth, alive and well.

And by the way, so are The Lone Ranger and Tonto. They've managed to survive the journey from print to radio, to TV and film, and now to the internet.

Go ahead, Google them, Kemosabe!

FROM WILD OATS TO OATMEAL

No, I'm not having oatmeal for breakfast because it lowers my cholesterol. I'm eating it because I like it. My mother's heritage was Scottish and she fed me oatmeal almost from birth, so it's home-food to me.

Shingo won't touch it. He's a ham and eggs man. But his Buddhist teacher, the late Reverend Kenko Yamashita, who was Soto Zen Bishop of North America, ate oatmeal every day, and, now that I think of it, he lived to be 88 years old. But that's not why I'm eating it.

Nor was all the hype about adding years to our lives the reason we quit smoking.

It wasn't smoking that was going to kill us, we reasoned, it was the no-smoking policies of airlines and airports and hotels and trains and subways and taxis and stores and restaurants we'd be faced with on a three week trip from Hawaii to Europe.

Both of us had smoked for fifty years. I was a three-pack a day addict and he wasn't much better. We each had those hacking coughs which sound so scary to non-smokers. But we'd smile at their concern, saying, "it's just a smoker's cough," as though a smoker's cough is less than lethal.

As the price of cigarettes rose, we went from buying them by the carton, to hand-making them using a little blue plastic machine.

13

If we ran out, we'd bargain with each other over who had to go out, right away, and get the cans of tobacco or the Zig-Zag filter tubes.

Before we even moved to Hawaii I researched which smoke-shop carried the products we'd be miserable without.

The hand-making and the paraphernalia added to the spell of smoking. We proudly showed guests our cigarette production line, though we snatched away and hid the makings from their children.

While we still lived in Los Angeles, a friend who'd recently kicked the habit came to our loft and, like a door-to-door religious zealot, gave us, unrequested, a book which he said had saved him from his evil ways. We thanked him, hypocritically, having no intention of ever opening the cover.

For the next ten years I used that book, *Allen Carr's Easyway To Quit Smoking*, to prop up my ashtray. But then, obeying some unconcious impulse, I brought it to Hawaii.

In 2008, Shingo had an art show scheduled in Sweden. That June we were to fly from Hilo to Honolulu, to San Francisco, to Chicago, to Stockholm, which, with layovers to make connections, was going to take the better part of two days in airports and on planes.

"We're going to go nuts without cigarettes," I told him. "By the time we get to Sweden we'll be ready to throttle each other."

"Maybe you need quit smoking," Shingo said, only half kidding.

"Maybe we should both quit," I countered. "We could start a couple of weeks before we leave. Wouldn't it be something not to be hooked on tobacco?"

Just like that, we agreed to try.

Shingo would use the patch and I'd use Wellbutrin, a tranquillizer which ex-smokers had recommended and which a doctor was only too happy to prescribe.

The patch worked perfectly for him. He didn't have cravings and was able to smoothly walk away from his years and years of puffing on cigarettes.

My tranquillizer, though, was too sedating. I didn't want to be stoned in Sweden or in the cities of Europe we planned to visit after Shingo's show.

In our medicine cabinet I happened to find four tablets of a mild prescription tranquillizer dated 1990, so long ago I'd forgotten why I had them. You could break these eighteen year old pills in two, so I tried one-half of one, and it worked. It took me past my desire for a cigarette which was stronger than usual that day. Meanwhile, I decided to finally open *Allen Carr's Easyway To Quit Smoking.*

But who'd believe that title? There's no such word as "easyway." And what could possibly be easy about getting out of a rut you've been in for most of your life?

Since we'd already started our quitting program, I skipped all the author's preliminaries and went right to the heart of the matter. And what he had to say was no different than behavior modification advice I'd heard from my old Zen teacher, Maezumi Roshi, in Los Angeles.

"You'll stop when you're finished," they both said. "You'll quit when you want to."

And we did want to.

So we quit.

It was that simple.

I still can't believe it.

Maybe "easyway" *should* be a word.

Only a few more stone-age pills went into it, and one stage of the patch, not three. Perhaps the most effective medicine was all the high-fives and big grins we lavished on each other as one day stretched into another with no relapsing. Before we even got on a plane we were free!

Our trip to Europe was to last three weeks, longer than we'd ever been away from our off-grid home.

In 2006, we'd gone to Japan for ten days, but during that time, one of our old Downtown friends, James Kendrew, came to stay.

Before we left, we coached him on how to manage the propane for the fridge and stove and hot water heater, and showed him how to interpret the voltmeter, and when to use the generator.

He had no problems with the off-grid stuff, but he couldn't say the same about the weather.

He'd intended to come to our isolated location to write, but being used to Southern California's perpetual sunshine, he almost lost it after five straight days of Hawaiian rainforest rain.

Once the sun came out, he went out. Never mind writing, let's hike, let's swim, let's escape.

Perhaps word of our occasionally inhospitable micro-climate had leaked, because we couldn't convince anyone from L. A. or elsewhere to house-sit this time around. Though weather doesn't stay the same from year to year, or even moment to moment here; and we'd been enjoying more sun than in past summers; and June, our travel month, was traditionally a dry one; we couldn't guarantee sunshine, so . . . no takers.

We wondered whether we could just lock up the house and walk away.

Except for the generator, we had no pets – no cats, no dogs – and no domestic animals, not even a chicken.

Did we need to do anything special?

Security, we felt, wasn't much of an issue. Our handful of neighbors are very vigilant. They know who comes and goes and aren't afraid to ask questions if they're not sanguine about a visitor.

A dramatic example of this island-style neighborhood watch took place in 2007 when two more of our Downtown friends arrived from Thailand: Michael Pigneguy and Vinh Luong.

They didn't get a car right away, but after a few days Shingo and I took them to Hilo to rent a vehicle. They got back to the house before we did and went to Shingo's art studio where they were staying.

One of our neighbors saw a strange car come down the road and not come back. He imagined someone was down here robbing us. He got his shotgun, and a friend of his, and the two of them came to investigate.

Hearing a truck pull into the driveway, our guest, Michael, came to the door of the studio.

"Where's Shingo!?" the neighbor demanded gruffly, as he and his buddy got out of the truck, not hiding the gun, and began to walk slowly, menacingly, towards the studio, protecting our property from thieves.

"I . . . I dunno," mumbled Michael, protecting Shingo from two guys with a gun who seemed to be "after" him.

Luckily, we pulled up at that very moment and were able to diffuse the situation.

After all the laughter was over, we thanked everyone for looking out for us, as we have for them, and will again in future, though in a more Buddhist way, without firearms.

Our main question about leaving the house for three weeks was whether or not to empty and turn off the refrigerator.

Would one propane tank go the distance? If so we'd leave the fridge running and not have to give away or throw away its contents.

Several experienced people confirmed what we thought we knew, that the answer was "Yes." One tank should last, no problem, since, with us out of town, it would only be used for the fridge.

So off we went, leaving the refrigerator on.

(If this were a television program, you'd now hear a musical cue: "Stingggg . . .")

Two days later we were in Sweden for Shingo's show, a group exhibition entitled *And The Clouds Are In Transition.*

Its theme was change, the temporary nature of existence, which has always been Shingo's guiding principle and theme.

As age creeps up on us, it's become our mutual guiding principal and theme. It goes like this:

"I guess we're going to have to die, huh?"

When Shingo was a child in his snow country home of Nagaoka, Japan, he'd pick up the ice on a puddle of water, so shiny and beautiful, but in a moment it had melted in his hand. He realized early that everything changes and, unlike most of us, accepted and even liked the idea. As he later learned, it was also a cornerstone of Buddhism.

Curated by gallery director Joanna Sandell, the show was mounted in the alternative artspace Botkyrka Konsthall, in Tumba, a short hop by commuter train from Stockholm's city center. Five international artists weighed in on the subject of change and transformation.

Shingo's *Hawaii Noon* prints were hung on two walls painted the rich blue-gray color of a rain-is-coming Hawaiian sky, which popped their sunbleached stillness, their peaceful silence: moments captured at high noon, before everything in the jungle starts moving and changing again.

Norwegian artist, Per Maning, whose work is in New York's Museum of Modern Art, had a blackout room built for him to show his film *The Perfect Stone,* a study of the life of a rock, which, as he sees it, is far from static.

American Eve Luckring combined a video loop with her poetry on shifting impressions in small town America.

Here's one of her observations:

> can't tell
> where one ends and the
> other begins
> smell of cut grass
> and gasoline

Britain's Emily Wardill showed a film in which the bells of St. Anne's Church in Limestone, London, told the time as it changed, ringing like the awareness bells in a Tibetan monastery.

And young Radoslaw Stypzcynski, from Poland, a wild-oat artist, if that means you're not exactly counting on selling your work, played a documentary he'd made about North Vietnamese immigrants living in post-Communist Warsaw: symbols of the inevitability of political change.

He also placed perhaps twenty brightly painted child-size stools throughout the konsthall, which children immediately took to and began to rearrange and play with, turning them into a castle or a dragon or whatever new form they dreamed up.

During the afternoon-long opening of the show, neither Shingo nor I had the urge to run outside for a smoke. Other people did, but not us. Things do change.

Not that I never had the urge again . . .

18

Sweden is a land of the midnight sun. During our trip, the sun stayed out until 11:00 p.m. An exceptional place for solar panels I thought, but it's not. In the winter, during Polar Night, it's dark for months on end, when the sun stays below the horizon. Nonetheless, Sweden plans to be the first oil-free economy. Already most of its energy comes from nuclear and hydro power.

After a few days of sightseeing around Stockholm, enjoying the hospitality of our Swedish hosts, we set off for Paris by train to see more friends from our Downtown L. A. Artists' District days.

Travelling on trains reminded us that we weren't youthful back-packers, but senior citizens with too much luggage. Standing in long lines in multiple stations changing multiple currencies to pay for tickets (some countries don't use the Euro), then standing in long lines to get the tickets, made us yearn for the much more efficient Japanese rail system.

The sounds-like-fun notion of spending a night in bunks onboard an express train out of Copenhagen turned sleepless when holidaying schoolboys in the next compartment stayed up all night drinking and playing cards. Hoisting heavy bags on and off overhead racks was just one more reason to wish we'd taken a plane to Paris.

All this, and our ultimate destination, made Shingo realize that he's now too old to live the fifth-floor-walkup garret-in-Paris artist's life he once dreamed of.

"Shikatanai. Cannot be helped," he told me. "Maybe I stay Hawaii!"

Laughing, we settled into the threadbare seats of a train which was also getting too old to cut the mustard. But at least it was heading in the right direction. We'd be having dinner in Amsterdam.

Viewing Europe from the windows of a train is an education in impermanence. Green fields stretch between cities, keeping their secrets of century after century of devastating wars.

How many young men and women, cousins from how many neighboring countries, ended their lives and were buried in the garden spots we were whizzing past, killed by arrows, swords, boiling oil, mustard gas, bullets, and bombs – killed by each other.

19

Like a trip through a hard-to-solve jig-saw puzzle where all the pieces look too much alike, building styles in each new country resembled the last, though rooflines, and gable shapes, and types of brick or stone might vary slightly. Barn door colors and silo colors changed from country to country, but without the dark reds of Sweden or the yolky yellows of Denmark, it was hard to say which country we were passing through, except when the windmills of Holland arose to dazzle us with their great age and off-grid usefulness.

Though it allowed us to see a lot of Europe, train travel was not at all elegant. There was no dining car on any of the trains we rode, no linen-covered tables with "railroad silver" flatware and wine glasses at every place-setting.

My father's father, a railroad station inspector in Canada, would have been so disappointed.

Just a bar-car with micro-waved food and stools around tiny tables was all that was offered in the name of dining. Consequently, when we reached Amsterdam, the site of a one-night stopover, I was determined to dine.

And dine we did at a restaurant famous for rijsttafel, literally "the rice table," which the Dutch brought back to Holland from their colonial adventures in the East Indies. Served with glossy white rice, it's a spicy Indonesian curried feast of many small dishes, each of which teases and pleases the palate. It's the leisurely sort of meal which makes you think of one final pleasure: smoking a cigarette.

But I put that out of my mind. At least I thought so.

We were planning to walk back to our hotel, but all that food made us logy, so we decided to take a streetcar instead. As we got to the platform, a tram was just pulling out and someone had thrown a newly lit cigarette on the cement median.

"Shingo, look!" I said, pointing at the fragrant smoke curling from the glowing-red end of a pure white filter-tipped ciggie. I may even have been leaning toward it with my hand out, when . . .

"Lynne!" Shingo said, pulling me away from there, "I SHOCK! You are not BUM!!!" Maybe not, but if he hadn't grabbed my arm I can't say what might have happened next.

In any case, our streetcar arrived and we got on it. The moment had passed.

Of course, you can smoke more than tobacco in Amsterdam. Every smoke shop has colorful signs for get-higher-and-higher brands of marijuana. I saw a liquor store selling alcohol laced with cocaine.

I mention this just to mention it. We agreed not to sample these products, even though they were legal. And this had nothing to do with our age – age has not made us prudish – it was just: who wanted to get higher and higher in a strange city when you had to rise early and be on a train?

Oh, alright, let's get real. Wasn't it I who didn't want to sow wild oats in Amsterdam? I've sown too many already.

And wasn't it I who insisted that my husband not sow as much as a single oat either? Hmmm . . . Maybe that's why he refused to kiss me goodnight.

The next day it was on to Paris, where we were met at the Gare Du Nord by a smiling young man, another treasured member of our Downtown L. A. family, Won Kim.

Won graduated from Pomona College in Claremont, California, with a degree in sports marketing; promoted bands and put on concerts while in school; opened a club upon graduation; helped launch Daewoo Motor America, a Korean car maker, in the U.S.; created a company which put ads on cars; and handled Samsung's Winter Olympics Sponsorship in Utah. None of these activities suggest his current occupation: he's a mime.

His art is perhaps less understood in the United States than it is in Europe and South America. Marcel Marceau may be the only mime we've ever heard of, but what Won has been studying and staging for the past ten years is not sketch comedy performed in whiteface.

The Pas de Dieux company in Paris, which he co-founded, directed by his wife Leela Alaniz, takes mime in a new direction, through body and mind, playing with muscular tension and relaxation, portraying in depth the thoughts within the actions of the actor, combining mime with dance, spoken word, and other disciplines, viscerally involving audiences regardless of the language they speak.

We were privileged to watch rehearsals for their show *Don Qui,* a cutting-edge retelling of the tale of Don Quixote, with Won as The Don.

Shingo doesn't cry easily, but I saw him dabbing away, moved not just by the good-beats-evil plot of the play itself, but pride in the professionalism of our dedicated friend, who, while living the impoverished garret-in-Paris life Shingo once wished for, had brought the impossible dream of becoming an artist into full flower for himself.

Needless to say, he's in top physical shape, not only from the grueling practice of his art, which equals a martial art in its requirements for training and discipline, but from walking up and down those five flights of stairs to his apartment.

Since Won, Leela, and company were immersed in preparations for upcoming performances of *Don Qui* at the Avignon Summer Festival, we would meet them and members of their troupe for dinner, but spent most of our days in Paris sightseeing.

The Louvre Museum was closed for renovations but the Musee D'Orsay was open and exhibiting paintings I've seen as reproductions all my life, from Cezanne's *Apples and Oranges* to Whistler's *Whistler's Mother,* the fourth most recognizable painting in the world.

Throughout the museum, groups of children, from first graders on up, could be found sitting on the floor in front of a painting or sculpture, asking and being asked questions by a teacher.

I had my own private instructor, Shingo Honda, who's well versed in art history. He made some himself in the 1970's, in his wild-oat days, as a participant in what is now known by art curators as the "Mono Ha" movement in Japan, "Mono Ha" meaning "The School of Stuff."

Let me tell you about two of his "Mono Ha" works, because it will provide an entrée into the off-the-wall mind of a twenty-four-year-old making internationally acknowledged art.

In a vast room in the Tokyo Municipal Museum, he installed a rough wooden floor using unfinished planks. Some of the planks were lifted slightly at one end, but not in any particular pattern. At times, Shingo would go in and change the boards. Did anyone notice?

In the Tokyo National Modern Art Museum he roped an enormous block of concrete to a column with a heavy ship's hawser. It seemed to be straining, wanting to get away. When the piece travelled to New York's Guggenheim Museum, there were no columns to rope it to. The concrete block had escaped its confinement.

Those installations, created so long ago with a bunch of wooden boards, and a concrete block and some rope, made the same point as the finely executed drawings of the Hawaiian rainforest at noon in his recent Swedish exhibition: nothing stays the same.

It's a fact which came home to us daily in our travels around the city which has nurtured some of the world's most talented artists.

Despite the number of avid students at the Orsay Museum, no one on the streets of Monmartre or Montparnasse seemed to know much about the artists who had once enlivened those precincts.

When Shingo stopped strangers and asked if they knew of the "Paris School – the "Ecole De Paris," or where Picasso, or Modigliani, or Tsuguharu Fujita had lived and worked, he received a blank stare or a Gallic shrug.

"They no remember," he'd say, downhearted, but perhaps he was asking the wrong people, in the wrong language: Shinglish.

Remembrance becomes an especially poignant issue for anyone who creates art which has been recognized in their lifetime.

They ask themselves, "Will it live on after my death? For how long? Will my work be earning millions at auction a century after I die? Or be gathering dust in someone's attic? Or have been ripped up and flung in the garbage the minute I'm in my grave?"

At the Pere Lachaise Cemetery, a big-draw tourist attraction, which was just a short walk from the apartment so generously loaned to us by Leela Alaniz, we saw how eminent people had tried to solve the immortality issue by building sturdy, striking, often very elaborate tombs.

Some graves had lifesize sculptures of their occupants, some featured powerful religious icons, some had fresh flowers "in perpetuity," but some had fallen into disreputable disrepair with broken statuary, rusted ironwork, and scarred, even graffiti'd, marble.

We learned that the cemetery gives 30 year leases on its gravesites and that, if an estate doesn't renew the lease, the cemetery has the right to remove a crumbling tomb and its occupant(s) and re-rent the site to someone else!

The ghosts of Pere Lachaise reaffirmed Shingo's childhood insight that nothing is forever.

But it's not as blatantly obvious there as it is at the Fushimi Inari Taisha, a Shinto shrine in Kyoto we'd been to on one of our trips to Japan.

There, people buy towering red gates to memorialize themselves or their loved ones, and these gates run, right next to each other, all the way up and around a mountain.

When you walk through the tunnel formed by these giant scarlet gates, you're tinted red by reflected color, and tinted further by the everlasting glory of the purchasers of the gates, some of which are now really ancient.

Until you come across a termite-riddled wooden stump, the remains of a gate which has disintegrated.

Or you come to a space between two gates. Uh oh! That gate is gone, making room for another immortality seeker. Or immortality sucker.

I don't want to suggest that we spent our entire time in Paris brooding over the inevitability of change or our relationship to oats. Thanks to the kindness of Won Kim, we saw theater and dance performances we'll never forget. We spent time strolling in gardens and parks; ate delicious dinners; window-shopped the bounty of boulangeries and charcuteries and patisseries, sampling only a smidgeon of their wares.

But impermanence and oatmeal returned as subjects for consideration when we finally took our leave of Won and Leela and their Pas de Dieux companions, and left Paris for Frankfurt, Germany, the first stop on our way back to Hawaii.

Wanting to take home a taste of Europe, I bought a jar of truffles, a jar of white asparagus, and a boxed assortment of European brandies in an airport shop. This would have to be carry-on, since our luggage had gone straight through from Paris to Hilo.

A customs official grabbed the white asparagus right away, citing the fact that it had more than a couple of ounces of liquid in the jar, a thing recently prohibited by security regulations.

Now that's impermanence! Here today – gone today!

Logically, he would next be bound to confiscate the truffles which were also surrounded by liquid, and the brandies, which were (Don't tell!) 100% liquid.

I couldn't understand why they would sell me these things in the airport and then take them away. I started crying, loudly, to Shingo's complete embarrassment.

I bawled at the customs official, "You're taking all my gifts! What am I going to give my friends? Boo hoo hoo hoo hoo!" And he, just trying to do his job, didn't. He let me though with the illicit items.

But I wasn't so lucky when we hit home.

There was this strange smell as we opened the door to the house.

It seemed to be coming from the kitchen, in the direction of the re-frigerator.

(Music Cue #2: "Stingggggg . . .")

I opened the fridge door, then slammed it shut. What I saw in there you don't want to know.

Apparently, one large tank of propane was not enough to keep it going for three weeks. Judging by the degree of disgusting, it must have gone on strike some time ago.

It took all of the following day to throw out yucky, smelly, moldy, dead things and clean the fridge and freezer.

Eventually, baking soda and bleach got the stink of change-as-the-natural-order-of-things out of the bottom section.

But, though I began to use the freezer again, it took a full three months to completely eliminate its lingering halitosis, that hint of "I used to be meat."

More bleach and scrubbing with soda, sachets of charcoal, bowls of coffee grounds, and bunches of ti leaves went into the rehab of the freezer.

Sniff, sniff ? Not quite . . .

Sniff, sniff? Go again . . .

Sniff, sniff? One more time . . .

I used every odor-eater anyone suggested, including that old fash-ioned, somewhat boring, but ultimately useful product, oatmeal.

THIS IS RETIREMENT?

In the nineteen-seventies and eighties, in the television industry, I was known as a "hyphenate," a writer-producer, a show-runner, on the long running hits *The Bob Newhart Show* and *The Love Boat*. In those show-must-go-on days, hyphen was a synonym for high pressure.

Here in Hawaii, a few decades later, there are new hyphens: off-grid dweller, author, and speaker. But there's no stress. I can hyphenate at my own pace.

Shingo had his hyphens here, too, as a fine artist and voluntary assistant priest. But in March 2009, change raised its shaved-bald head when the abbot of Hilo's Taishoji Soto Zen Temple, Reverend Shinryu Akita, retired.

He went to Saipan, where it's hotter than Hawaii (it's hotter than Hades) not to relax and take it easy after a lifetime of service to others – he went to take care of a shrine he built years ago to memorialize the thousands who died on Saipan in WWII: 43,000 Japanese military and 12,000 Japanese civilians, some of whom were encouraged to commit suicide by jumping off cliffs as defeat seemed certain; 3,500 Americans; and at least 900 Saipanese, including infants and the elderly, all lost their lives.

Rev. Akita was 80-something and had recently had a heart attack, but that didn't change his plans.

He's the real Buddhist deal, a Bodhisattva, rarely encountered, who walks his talk, and will spend every remaining moment of his life doing for others, so when he asked Shingo, who'd been volunteering as his assistant for several years, to take over as the "interim" minister of the Hilo temple while the Board of Directors looked for a new resident minister, Shingo was on the spot.

Though he wouldn't be required to live at the temple, he'd be performing services at once-a-month events such as Buddha's Birthday, or Buddha's death day; funerals, and the many memorial services which take place starting on the day after a funeral, then on the 7th day, the 35th, the 49th, the 100th, the 1 year, 3 year, 7 year, 13th, 17th, 23rd, 27th, 33rd, and 50th year anniversaries of a person's passing, all of which required sermons, pronounced by Shingo as "salmons."

He'd also be expected to visit temple members in hospital, go to every board meeting, and attend conferences of the wider Buddhist community. If someone was dying he could be summoned to their bedside at any time of the day or night.

It was a full-time job and he'd be on call 24 hours.

Shingo tried to beg off, but how can you say "no" to someone you revere?

He tried "I'm an artist, I have to make art," but it didn't work. He tried, "I haven't studied at a monastery in Japan," "I can't read or write English," and even the over-used "I'm unworthy," but Reverend Akita didn't budge: there was no one else who could step in and allow him to get on with his Saipan plans.

"Shikatanai. Cannot be helped," Shingo told me as he accepted the position.

This struck me as way too humble and not the whole story. I thought he was going to love being the temporary minister of Taishoji Temple. Why? Because he loves the people there.

As for me, I had no intention of filling, temporarily or otherwise, the role of "oku-san," or minister's wife, so ably filled by Mrs. Akita, who, when not teaching formal flower arranging, laundered kitchen towels, swept pathways, took care of endless temple tasks.

This Is Retirement?

Not that I have an aversion to the work she did so well, but there are a limited number of days and years left in which to write, and write is what I plan to do with them. Board members kindly understood this and divided up the oku-san chores among themselves.

But if I could escape the job of temple wife, I couldn't duck the duties which came up unexpectedly.

Reverend and Mrs. Akita had hardly left the Big Island on their way to Saipan, when Shingo's cell-phone rang one afternoon. I heard him speaking to Taishoji Temple's president, Walter Tachibana, agreeing to do something priestly.

After he got off the phone he explained that a temple member's relative had died in Las Vegas and they wanted a priest to perform "makuragyo" for him.

This is a purification ceremony with incense and candlelight and chanting which should take place as soon as possible after someone passes away. It usually happens at the person's deathbed, but in this extraordinary case, Shingo was asked to perform the ceremony, long distance, over the phone.

He was given a number for the funeral home in Vegas which was handling the arrangements, and called it, but was told by a switchboard operator that the facility was closed. Then, before he could say another word, she said, "I'll transfer you."

I could hear him having trouble understanding and being understood, so I loitered. Soon he handed me the phone, asking, "Could you help?"

"First of all, who am I speaking to?" I asked the person who'd answered.

"This is 'Affordable'," said a pleasant male voice.

"Uh, Affordable what?" In Las Vegas, "Affordable" could be a wedding chapel, a divorce court, a motel, a bakery . . .

"Affordable Mortuary," the nice man said.

"Oh, good. And is Mr. X with you?"

He took a moment to check his roster, then, "Yes, he's here," he said.

29

I explained that my husband was a Buddhist priest and that he needed to chant for the late Mr. X.

"Okay," said the nice man, "The only problem is, we don't have a P.A. system."

"Then," I gently inquired, "is there any possibility you could bring him to the phone?"

Without hesitation, this upbeat person, who must have seen and heard just about everything connected with death, said, "Sure, I'll have my guys bring him down right now."

While we were waiting for Mr. X, we lit a candle and incense, placed a pretty flower, and readied the bell and small drum which would accompany the ceremony, taking place, impromptu, with our dinner table as an altar.

When Mr. X arrived, Shingo told the mortuarian that there would be three bells to start and two to end the ceremony: after that, he should come back on the line and they could end their conversation.

Shingo rang the opening bells and began to chant the soothing Japanese syllables into the phone and play a tiny drum as punctuation. I'm still imagining, with a tear in my eye, how this looked at the other end.

It was beyond moving for us, this long-distance last rite, Shingo's first as a solo minister, because of the can-do attitude of a perfect stranger in Las Vegas. In accepting our thanks, he made it sound like just another day at Affordable.

After that, Shingo was in ministerial full swing. He's well trained in Japanese Zen Buddhist ceremonial etiquette and can do a funeral, a monthly celebration, or memorial service without much assistance, except when it comes to the "salmon," which, in Hilo, must be delivered in English.

Imagine yourself as an immigrant to the United States from a foreign country, where not only is the language different, but the handwriting is, too – there are three styles of pictographic writing in Japan. Imagine that you've come to the U. S. at age 40, too late to learn English as children do, by ear; too late, or too old, or too obstinate, to thoroughly study the language you're mainly going to be operating in for the rest of your life.

You expect to wing it, and you do, quite successfully, for twenty-six years, never dreaming that some day you'll have to give a speech – not just one speech, many speeches; speech after speech after speech; in the absolutely unintelligible English language.

Imagine that you marry a writer who loves English, but who has to admit it's impossible to understand. When you ask her to explain why certain words have the same sound but very different spellings, you wish you could get a better answer out of her than "Ummm..."

Why is it "ghost" and "toast"? "Goose" and "juice"? "Sandal" and handle"? "Rope" and "soap"? "Eight" and "plate"? "Troll" and "bowl"?

And how about "bite," "slight," "white KNIGHT"? "Pear," "chair," and "dare"? "Hi" and "high"? "Hire" and "higher"?

What about "sled", and "bread", and "said"? "Sleigh," "today," "obey"? "Flew", "flu", "flue" ???

"Ummm . . ."

Now, imagine you're trying to pronounce these words as you see them: "guhost," "toe-ast," "beetay," "breeyad," "joowikay." Try "neighborhood."

Don't forget that you tend to transpose the letters "L" and "R", "V" and "B", "H" and "F", and that "th" sounds to you like "sss" and "er" sounds like "ahh".

For you, "first" becomes "fast" and "light" is "right." "Faith" is "face." "Earth" is "ass." A "horse" is a "force." A "fork" is a "hork." "Legend" could be "raisin," or was that "raging"?

"Rubber" is "lava" and "lover" sounds like "robber." A "parrot" is a "palate." A "pilot" is a "pirate." "Liberation" comes out "revela-tion." And don't even try to pronounce "ladder."

With all this in mind, let's see you write and deliver an esoteric Zen Buddhist sermon in English that will inspire, uplift, and inform your audience.

For Shingo it was more than a job, it was lots of jobs.

To begin with, he'd write his sermon in Japanese, then give it to our friend Yoko Gussman – she did this as a kindness – for direct transla-tion into English.

31

Then it came to me for further English interpretation and scanning for words like "realm," that Shingo would never be able to say.

Then it went back to him for its first out-loud English reading, with me correcting pronounciation. He wrote all the hard-to-read parts in phonetic Japanese above the English words.

After that, he rehearsed aloud at least three times.

Then came the dress rehearsal with last-minute notes about pronounciation and clarity.

Finally, he gave the talk at Taishoji Temple.

Even with all this good prep, on his first time out Shingo asked his listeners, five family members assembled for a memorial service, whether they understood his sermon.

They shook their heads and wrinkled their noses. It was a "No."

But this "No," had no animosity to it, expressed, as it was, in a town where many people's grandparents or parents, first generation Japanese immigrant sugar or coffee workers, sounded just like Shingo.

It included a laugh, which typifies the Hilo attitude: "If it's no fun, we're not doing it."

It produced a laugh from Shingo, whose smile is enough to make you his friend.

Nevertheless, it was back to square one in the "salmon" department.

Easier and more comfortable were his trips to hospitals where the folks he was attending were often over 90. Taishoji people tend to live long, productive, lives and only enter hospital on the last legs of their journeys. Shingo would sing old Japanese songs with them, songs from their childhood and his, and have them feeling right at home.

But every request to go to a hospital had us both in a state of alarm. Who was sick? Were they going to make it? Were they going to die?

Losing even one of them meant losing an inspirational, culturally knowledgeable, often very funny, how-can-I-help-you, never-leave-until-the-work-is-done, member of the community. We wanted more, not less, of them.

We also wanted more, not less, of us, though each hospital experience, and the stories Shingo told when he got home, brought us face to face with our own fears: that the style of our deaths may be something

32

we have no control over; the absolute reality that we're running this race at a quickening pace and will have to cross the finish line one of these days.

During all this time, my busy husband, whom some of our less-reverent friends now referred to as "holy man," still had to contend with the regular maintenance of our off-grid home, taking propane tanks to be re-filled and re-installing them every few weeks; making sure there was gas for the generator; refilling 5 gallon bottles of drinking water in Keaau; changing filters for the catchment water; checking the level of distilled water in the batteries for the solar system and filling them up when necessary; changing the oil in the generator and cleaning the air filter. He brought home truckloads of branches left on the roadside by County tree-trimmers to use as kindling in our wood-stoves. He stacked the logs we bought from George Indie. He bought and shovelled truckloads of gravel into the potholes on our lumpy country road. He took the laundry to the laundromat in Hilo. He chopped down overhanging tree limbs on our street which might prevent FedEx or UPS from coming to the house.

And he was still painting, getting ready for a show in L. A. and another in Japan in May of 2010.

Nevertheless, he devoted more and more time to his sermons. Because of them he was learning to read some English, and properly pronouncing difficult words such as "patriarchs," "atonement," "purifies," "encourages," "refuge," "exalted," "virtue," "precepts." "Tranquility" became one of his favorites.

Sometimes a service was already written in English and he was only required to present it. But still, he wanted to know what it meant.

At one point he had to say the word "composure." Asking about it, he waved an imaginary baton.

"No, that's composer," I said. "Composure is similar to tranquility."

"Oh, that's me," he said, happily. "I am composure tranquility guy."

"Right!" I agreed, telling just the tiniest white lie.

Throughout his tenure, everyone at the temple was completely supportive. At first, during services, you could find his audience on the edge of its collective seat, worrying whether Shingo was going to make it through some English sentence. Then, like grandparents, they'd exhale a joint sigh of relief when he did, and settle back into their pews. At least the prevailing tension during "salmons" kept most members from falling asleep.

In the past, Shingo had always told me that his religion was "not for sale." He wanted to volunteer as a guide and assistant, but never receive a salary from Zen.

But, as we know, things change, and it must be said that the small salary he received for almost a year as Taishoji's interim minister was helpful to us in a worldwide financial downturn when very few people were buying his paintings.

It was also a help to have the use of the temple's car, and gas to go with it, when our truck only got 16 miles to the gallon and the price of gas was soaring.

Meanwhile, I'd say the temple got a deal. For close to a year they didn't have to pay a live-in minister's higher salary and expenses, including electricity, water, phone, cable TV, health insurance, moving costs, and, perhaps, new furnishings.

Do you see where I'm heading with this? Reverend Honda was an affordable minister.

Then in February 2010, the new English-speaking resident minister arrived in Hilo and Shingo went back to being a very occasional assistant priest. Though life without a full-time, heavier, hyphen is much less intense, I think he misses it.

THIS IS A RECESSION?

I was reading a new-wave green magazine which was full of gloom and doom about the 2008-2009 recession. According to the story, one way out of the short-sighted selfishness, the "I'm making billions and you're not" inequality, the tax and spend on war-war-war government; a way around those inter-locked, impenetrable, economic influences, would be to create a "gift economy."

The idea was to detour around money, tiptoe past the powers-that-be: to share and trade home-grown food with neighbors and friends; share home-made cooking, canning, and baking; to never go empty-handed to anyone's home; to offer your expertise without stinting; and to never think of give and take. All this and more would come back to you without asking or expecting.

The newly coined name "gift economy" made me giggle. By any name (aloha?), or no name at all, this behavior has been a way of life in the Hawaiian Islands forever.

And it's still going on, recession or no recession.

It's "What can I bring?" squared.

It's too many bananas from somebody's tree; it's more fresh-from-the-garden eggplant and green beans than you can eat in a week; it's fish caught this morning AND smoked pork AND boiled peanuts; it's the multi-cultural riches of Hawaii coming to your front door.

The gift economy already existed on our almost uninhabited country road. But before we could really say we participated in it we needed more neighbors. And we needed our own garden.

In mid-recession, we got them.

One of the reasons I wanted to move to Hawaii was to take a survival stance, to go back to the land and grow much of our own food. But once we got here, I made too many false starts, losing my tiny crops to too much rain, the wrong soil, slugs, cutworms, wild pigs: in whatever way it was possible to flop, I flopped, giving me new respect, even awe, for food, and farmers who know how to grow it to maturity.

My most obvious mistake was trying to grow vegetables and fruits as though living in sunny, dry – it's a desert – Southern California. Here, some plants need an umbrella.

So I got them one.

For the heck of it, I looked up "clear plastic umbrellas" on the internet, found them, bought a few, sawed off the handles, and attached them to sticks which I shoved into the ground.

Did it work? It did. Cucumber and eggplant, which used to damp off in the rain, now have their own personal parasols. They're growing! And the umbrellas look whimsical in the garden.

Knowing no better, I planted things at our place that knowledgeable people might not.

"Papayas? You can't grow papayas up there – too cold," I was told. But, by some stroke of luck, at 2,300 feet above sea level, five papaya trees are producing fruit. Small – *very* small. But tasty. Likewise, white pineapples, grown from lopped off tops, are now thigh high and not only fruiting but looking decorative in our front yard.

Bananas are burgeoning, too, which is not as big a deal. They seem to flourish in all kinds of conditions. Though our temperature can drop, as it did this year, to 52 degrees Fahrenheit, the bananas didn't seem to care.

Figs are figging. When the tree I planted was only a few feet high it started producing fruit. How illogical. A fig is from a Mediterranean climate: more like L. A. But somehow, here, on a teenage tree, are six figs. I'm hovering over them wondering when to pick. The one I did pick tasted like cardboard, not ripe enough, but I'm waiting and watching and gently pinching the rest.

Hydroponic lettuce has been successful from the beginning. It grows in six window boxes outfitted for still-water hydroponics, sitting on shelves on the side of the house. A mini-system, it grows just as much salad as we want to eat.

The secret to raising food in the soil, it seems, is drainage. And the secret to drainage is cinders. Every fruit tree and every vegetable on our land is now growing in a bed of shiny black chunks of The Goddess Pele's volcano.

The other secret, which is no secret, is sun. Much of my past far-merette failure was attributable to a dearth of golden rays. The best place for sun at our house is on the front lawn, so any garden we put there must be attractive as well as practical: it ought to enhance the landscape and grow food.

With this in mind, at one end of the lawn, Shingo dug three ditches, fifteen feet long by three feet wide, by three feet down, which we framed with wood painted to match the house. Between each ditch is a strip of lawn wide enough for a rider-mower. It's the reverse of a raised bed garden. It's deep instead of high, and has no fluffy soil. We mixed some of the clay soil we dug up with bags of cinders, then enriched the beds with well-rotted compost and manure.

These long beds are now growing nine varieties of Japanese vegetables and herbs: the leafy greens komatsuna and mibuna; the eat-the-whole-thing root vegetables daikon and kabu (white turnip); the fragrant flavor enhancers shungiku, mitsuba, and oniony rakyo. Soy is a new experiment. Ask me next year how it did.

Not to be outdone, Western carrots, asparagus, green beans, green onions, and leeks are growing, too, as are Thai basil, Vietnamese mint, and that global ingredient cilantro.

Tomatoes are a total bust. They'd do better in a greenhouse, but I'm too stingy to buy or build one. Approaching this decision like an actuary, it would take too many years worth of harvested vegetables to equal the up-front cost of a good looking greenhouse, more years than we're likely to have.

But even if we're fated to live long enough to amortize the cost, I'm just as happy with cinder-filled ditches and a few umbrellas. Friends who have greenhouses are always running around with shadecloth and fans when they get too hot. Who can be bothered?

Fertilizer turns out to be a main ingredient for a basket-full-of-goodies-as-seen-on-the-cover-of-the-seed-catalogue garden. Okay, I'm a moron, but I never thought to fertilize during our first couple of years here. It's so green everywhere you look, and tropical flowers, tame and wild, are constantly blooming, so I didn't understand that the soil lacks nutrients needed by veggies and fruits. They're leached out by heavy rains. Now I watch the rain guage and, after every 12 inches of rain, sprinkle organic fertilizer to give our food some food.

It also helps to plant viable seeds saved from the year before by me or a seed vendor. Seeds I've been hoarding in already-opened packages since Adam ate the apple probably won't sprout. For rare seeds, though, it's worth a try.

The fifth and most important encouragement for the vegetable garden is a lack of pigs. I must gratefully admit I haven't seen a wild pig for more than a year which is why I'm harvesting anything at all. Even a piglet could dig up the whole garden in a single night.

That's another reason for the cinders. Theoretically, the glassy-sharp cinders will hurt a pig's snout and give it a strong hint to root elsewhere. But cinders aren't stopping pigs from coming. I think it's hunters and more dogs in the area.

There's been no need, lately, for me or Shingo to stand at the door barking loudly, imitating big mean dogs, to try and scare away a family of pigs. Which never worked anyway. The pigs would look right at us and go on rooting as if to say, "Get a life!"

The amount of produce grown here will never replace the farmer's market where papayas in season are six for a dollar. We'll still need the supermarket, too, (you can't grow toilet paper), but it's fascinating, and fun to defy the odds and grow food in a rainforest. These days, some part of every meal is home grown.

There's only one thing missing from our Madame-Pele-meets-Mother-Earth Hawaiian homestead picture and that's chickens. We both imagined raising them when we moved here, but having had a frustrating failure during our first year, we've held off – uh huh, that was us blossoming in big red welts, itching and scratching, allergic to chicken-mite bites.

It would be nice to see chickens toddling about, and even nicer to have some eggs. But what about those mites? Frankly, I'm scared, as in "chicken." So chickens have become a dream – Shingo's, not mine. When the subject comes up, I procrastinate. It's "Let's talk chickens some other time."

Everything about off-grid existence teaches self-sufficiency but, as we now know well, you need other people every step of the way.

Following the unremitting law of nature, the close-by neighbors who saw us through our first-year baby steps are gone – things change.

Big Dave Little, the next door guitarist/Mr. Fixit/computer tech, returned to California to travel with a young rock band and hasn't come back. Auntie Jean Nihau, who lived off-grid for thirty-five years and personally established a school for orphans in Pakistan, passed away from a stroke not long after lightning struck her house.

Uncle Charlie Nihipali, his wife Gina, and cousin Felix have all moved, too, leaving us with memories of Charlie's priceless stories, Felix's handcarved tiki still smiling in our garden and his discarded turquoise van rusting away in a nearby meadow, but nobody to help spread gravel on the road.

Soon, however, new neighbors entered our lives, though they don't all live on the street. Some live above or below us, but we met because of their connection with a young man who's clearing a lot and building a house at the corner.

Men and women, they range in age from sixty-odd down to their twenties, and any job that needs doing can pretty much be done expertly by one of them.

Build a house? Train a dog? Drive a semi? Repair a roof? Install a car radio or wall-to-wall carpet? Work with at-risk teenagers? Landscape a hotel? Write a grant petition? Teach salsa dancing?

Unfortunately, during recessionary times, their skills were under-used, with work hard to find, catch as catch can. Nobody was exactly rolling in money.

That's why the idea of a weekly potluck was such a good one, sug-gested by Taylor De Court, the twenty-six year old at the corner.

We'd meet at his unfinished house every Tuesday night at six, sit in his carport, rain or shine, and feed and amuse each other.

Dinner was always over-the-top, with favorite dishes, like Doug Winston's clam dip appetizer or his killer guacamole appearing often by popular demand. Shrimp and cocktail sauce was the finger-food contribution of neighbor "Ski" alias Robert Stefanski.

The barbecue would be on, and fish, steak, and mouthwatering do-mestic pork, tenderized with lots of garlic, would be cooked by neighbor James-known-as-Seamus Dawn, and served in slices so that everyone could enjoy them all. Other friends brought other food. And let's not forget the beer.

You know how it is with a potluck: nothing's planned but every-thing seems to go with everything. Who'd have thought my eggplant caponata would enhance the best smoked wild pig on the island, sent by neighbor Rita Pragana, who could never attend our Tuesday gather-ings because of her schedule as a forest ranger?

Where else could you enjoy Kris Thario's handrolled, handfilled, handcrimped, homemade ravioli; or Tony Pothul's seafood won ton with sweet and sour sauce; or Meera De Court's Caesar salad; sample all the entrees, then end with home-grown fruit or Kris's decadent brownies, all served on paper plates, with plastic utensils, off a table made from a piece of plywood sitting on three buckets?

There was hardly ever a scrap of food left over. You had to feel sorry for the dogs and cat.

After dinner we'd play a game, often *"Pictionary,"* with two teams. This worked for Shingo, who, as an artist, was good at drawing, though someone usually had to whisper what the English word meant that he was supposed to draw.

Neighbor Tony is from Scotland and has a thick Scottish brogue, hard to understand. Shingo loved it when people would yell at Tony, "Speak English!"

Ski Stefanski is a retired submariner who once went to the North Pole in a submarine.

"How much did that cost us?" I asked him, taxpayer's tongue in cheek, eliciting a story about how, on another North Pole trip, one of a convoy of subs was damaged by ice and had to limp to Pearl Harbor to go into drydock. So the answer to my question was "Many many millions."

A potluck was a way to party together, and save money. It was cheaper and easier to make one dish to share than for each person to make an entire meal. Grilling a variety of foods on one barbecue saved cooking fuel. And the co-operation, good will, and friendship that grew from this regular event created a "hood."

The gatherings were a boon for all of us in terms of food and fun and in finding help for any need. But, as folks began to get work and be busier, the weekly event wore itself out and became an occasional party at other people's houses, though some of the regulars continued to meet at Taylor's and work out every morning to get rid of their potluck pot bellies.

In every economic downturn, writers put forth theories about how to fix the world. *Time Magazine*, in a March 2010 special issue entitled *Ten Ideas For The Next Ten Years*, featured an article, *The Dropout Economy*, written by journalist Reihan Salam.

As "dropouts" he imagined millions of families living off the grid, and powering their homes and vehicles with dirt-cheap portable fuel cells.

Industrial agriculture, he thought, would inevitably sputter under the spiraling costs of water, gasoline, and fertilizer. Then, networks of small farmers "using sophisticated techniques with ancient Mayan know-how" would build "alternative food systems."

Many of the young, he wrote, would create a new underground in largely untaxed communes and co-ops that would passively resist the power of the granny state while building their own little utopias. Private homes, he opined, would increasingly give way to co-housing with shared kitchens and common areas and neighborhood watch duty.

This "dropout economy" article made me chuckle even more than the one about the "gift economy."

First of all, show me the dirt-cheap portable fuel cells we're all going to be using in the next ten years to run our homes and vehicles.

From what I can see on the internet, fuel cell technology doesn't promise to be cheap or widely available. It's currently limited to small science-fair projects, large commercial power-backup installations, and, here and there, a cartoonish futuristic car.

It's exciting to know that hydrogen fuel cells were the primary power source for manned U.S. space missions but our house is not a rocket. And, as one website pointedly inquires: "Where you gonna get your hydrogen?"

The golf-cart batteries that store the solar power for our house are anything but portable. They're huge and heavy. Though fed by solar energy, they still need plenty of extra juice from the generator, which is gas fueled and therefore at the mercy of the King of Saudi Arabia.

Regarding food: home gardens, and farmer's markets, on The Big Island, and tail-gait vendors by the side of the road selling freshly caught fish, lobsters in season, poi, and "smoke meat," already challenge imported supermarket fare, but they're hardly building alternative food systems.

These gardeners, farmers, fishers, and hunters are go-it-alone types who just happen to be eating, or giving away, or selling what they just grew or caught. Unlike a supermarket, they may not be there tomorrow and they don't have everything-all-the-time. You can't count on them for a mango, or a yam, or a tomato, though if they've got one, it'll probably taste pretty good.

About untaxed communes, co-housing, community kitchens and common areas, viewed as little utopias: for three years in the late 1980's I lived in a Zen Center which offered all of the above, and I just have one question:

"Who left their dirty dishes in the kitchen sink AGAIN?"

After seventy years of lifestyle experimentation, I believe utopia's neither a place nor a system, it's a mind-set of appreciating what you've got, and saving a little something for somebody else.

Electrical engineer Rich Reha exemplified this way of living: after crawling around under our house to wire and install Rich's Switch in our bedroom, he said there'd be no charge. This kind man had decided he'd never take money for his services again. Feeling privileged to live an abundant life in Hawaii, he wanted only to give something back.

Likewise, even on a week with no pot lucks, I can still bake an extra loaf of banana bread from the big hand of cooking-only bananas given to us by Russell and Valerie Nakao, to give to neighbor James-known-as-Seamus Dawn, who can still come over and fix the lock on the trunk of our car, which he just did.

Oh, I forgot to tell you that in 2009, having returned the temple's automatic van, we traded in our manual-transmission truck for an automatic car. This was partly because of our age.

The manual truck involved too much heavy clutch and gear-shift wrangling. And we'd been spoiled by the ease of handling the temple's automatic van. Also, we thought it would be good to save money by driving a car, which would be thriftier on gas.

They say, as you get older, your brain cells slough off, and we must have sloughed off quite a few because instead of trading up, we traded down.

We bought our new/old Honda Passport in one afternoon, and realized later that it guzzles almost as much gas as our traded-in truck, and it's two years older. The mileage was a little lower but that didn't stop the car from having one problem after another from the moment we bought it.

First, the key wouldn't come out of the ignition. So we replaced the ignition. Then the key wouldn't come out of the new ignition. It would stop the engine but wouldn't pull out of the lock, but then it would, but then it wouldn't.

The service department at Big Island Honda later identified the trouble as being not with the ignition at all, but with the gear shifter. But nobody knew what to do about it.

Since we now had one key to run the car and another to lock it from the outside, we decided we didn't care if the key got stuck in there. Of course, once we stopped caring, it stopped acting up.

Next a belt snapped and sent wire all through the engine's moving parts to the tune of a $1,000 cleanup and replacement.

Then it had a flat and needed two new tires.

Then the trunk lock failed so we couldn't use the trunk. After Big Island Honda repaired it with a wink and a prayer, they stated that, without buying more parts for it, it would probably fail again. I didn't, and it did.

Big Island Honda wants $115 to do a "diagnostic," in other words they want a hundred bucks just to say hello, after which there's the cost of parts and labor.

I bought the necessary trunk parts from them, but neighbor James aka Seamus, volunteered to fix the lock. He's the same good neighbor who selected and installed a car radio/cd player for us when the new/old one refused to work.

Unfortunately, he couldn't replace the leaking radiator. For that we had to go to a specialist.

So, though we're already off the grid, and we're part of a so-called gift economy, and part of an underground economy, if you will, which saw us through the recession in style, we still need money.

We had to buy those tires. And replace the snapped fan belt. And buy trunk lock parts, and a new radiator.

There's no cheap portable fuel cell yet, so we still need gas for the car and the generator. We still need propane for the fridge and stove and water heater, and prices are still going up.

Although we're living what some describe as an alternative life-style, I'm still a capitalist, making money from dividends, and interest, and capital gains on investments. We're still entrepreneurs, selling our wares: paintings and books. We're enjoying most, if not all, of the comforts of the rich world.

44

But I think anyone who suggests that people, especially North Americans, will rush in great numbers to copy our way of life, or something even simpler, is smoking a funny pipe.

Very few, I'll wager, will try to grow their own food. Even in Hawaii we have things called seasons and you can't grow much in some of them.

Nor will they attempt to trade food or services for all their needs. The reason humans invented money was to provide an easier medium of exchange.

Nor will they move to communes or leave their comfortable homes for co-housing with a shared kitchen and common area. And neither will Shingo and I. We're, all of us, much too pampered and individualistic.

And to that, I raise my glass. It's our selfish qualities, our unquenchable desires, and our innovative abilities which will motivate us to pull ourselves, and the world, out of what, for our household, has been a what-me-worry recession.

We just need to remember never to take it to the "I'm a billionaire and you're not" stage, unless, like Bill Gates and Warren Buffet, we're planning to give most of it away and save the world.

No, I take that back. Those billionaire boys at Google and Facebook have already changed the world. As has Oprah Winfrey. They deserve to enjoy any penny they get.

WEALTH IN THE BOONIES

Heh, heh, heh! *The Hawaii Tribune-Herald* just announced on its front page "WATER RATES TO RISE UP TO 8 PERCENT."

Do we care? Nope.

As mentioned, except for drinking water, the water we use for bathing and dishwashing and toilet flushing arrives as rain, slides down the roof into gutters, and proceeds to the catchment, where it's stored until needed.

On demand, it's filtered, and can be heated, for use. Aside from the propane used to make it hot and the filters we buy to filter it, it's free.

It doesn't dent the budget and that's one goal of moving off the grid: to live, as comfortably as possible, unaffected by the vagueries of "the system" without going broke. Catchment water fills the bill.

Unless there's no rain.

In our second year off-grid, another member of our Downtown family, Youn Woo Chaa, arrived from Los Angeles, in sunny October, with a three-bedroom tent and six other people, one of whom was his two-year-old son, planning to stay for a couple of weeks. With lots of after-swim showers and baby baths plus dishwashing for nine, we soon began to run short of water. On a Thursday, it became obvious that unless we had some consistent heavy rain we'd need to buy some.

I was anxious because ordering water wasn't easy.

46

You had to call on a Monday at 8:00 a.m., keep trying until you got through, place your order, then wait for delivery on a first-come first-served basis.

Monday was four days away: four days before we could even call and order. And who knew how many days it would be before the water arrived?

We would very probably run out.

What would we do? Go to a hotel?

But I need not have worried. That night, one of our guests, Kang SanEh, a chart-topping South Korean rock singer, sat on the back steps and sang a hypnotic Korean rain chant. As he crooned his second chorus, the big fat drops began to fall and soon became a cloudburst, arriving to howls of welcome.

With more encouragement from him, it rained every night after that and we never did have to buy water. (The three-bedroom tent leaked but nobody complained.)

We've only bought water once since then and that was with no guests, just a month-long drought in January 2010.

Hoping for rain, but without SanEh's special gifts, we got down to a few inches of water in the bottom of the catchment tank, proving that we're much more relaxed about off-grid logistics than we used to be. But by then, the water-ordering rigamarole had changed. You could order on any day and the truck would come the next morning.

We filled the tank to overflowing with 4,500 gallons for $183. Naturally, it poured rain the next day – that's a rainforest running gag.

Until Spring of 2010, we were still filling five gallon bottles with drinking water at a water machine in Keaau, spending about $10 a month. Even so, the cost of off-grid water has been negligible.

Of course, there's a catch to that. When it's consistently raining, you don't get as much electricity out of your solar panels.

In 2007 Hawaii's electric bills went up by 13%. We hee-hee'd over that one at the time, but maybe we shouldn't be too cocky about our electrical self-sufficiency since we've so far spent about $14,000 to make it happen and probably aren't done yet.

We recently put in four more solar panels so we're not as dependent on the generator.

We can now use Shingo's lifeline, the rice cooker, even on a somewhat rainy day, without cranking up the adorable machine.

We can use the oven, which, though it's propane fired, has an electric on/off element that gobbles electricity. I made pizza the other night, requiring 475 degrees, without the generator running in the background.

But if we want to bake and make rice on the same day? There'd better be a lot of sun. And if we should want to vaccuum, use a hairdryer, or make toast at the same time, no amount of sun can handle it.

And if the sun doesn't come out at all? That's the reason to adore the generator.

Propane for making hot water and running the stove and fridge is pricey. We've been spending more than $100 a month on it. And still Shingo has to schlep the tanks from home to filling station and back, which is starting to pall.

In our first year off-grid we looked into home delivery of propane by The Gas Company, but couldn't accept the necessity of a huge, ugly, elephant-gray tank which had to be visible from the road, and many expensive feet of galvanized pipe, installed by an even more expensive licensed plumber, to bring the gas to the house. We estimated it would cost a few thousand dollars to install, be costly to fill, and we'd hate the look of it. Like raising chickens, it became one of those Scarlett O'Hara issues: "I'll think about that tomorrow."

Gas for the generator and the car, which has gone from $3.70 per gallon to a record $4.51 in the first four months of 2011, is now running us close to $200 a month, depending on how often we go to town or drive around the island.

When fuel prices go down elsewhere in the United States, they don't go down much in Hawaii, where every drop of refined oil must come in by ship, especially on the Big Island where it has to travel farther.

So can we reduce our use of imported fuels? With the new solar panels we'll save around $50 worth of generator gas each month in the long sunny days of summer, but, unfortunately our car won't run on the sun, and neither will the water heater, stove, or fridge (where are those doggone fuel cells when you need them?).

It then becomes a matter of quality of life. Will we deprive ourselves of a trip to Kona or the beach, or a nightly hot bath? Not on your money-grubbing life.

At our age, we deserve our perks. Though money is a consideration, a rather cruel cliché is tapping us on the shoulder: "You can't take it with you."

Since I was a teenager I've wondered about money: "How much is enough?" And, if a yearly figure or an overall sum could be established, what would I be willing to do for it?

I observed that my parents, though they had severe financial ups and downs, never went hungry, always had shelter, never were short of anything really important. But their own delusions about who they were and what they needed meant they always had too little.

In Hollywood, on *The Love Boat*, I worked for Aaron Spelling who built himself the most expensive house in America with over a hundred rooms and a bowling alley in the basement. He used to bring in truckloads of snow at Christmas to delight his two small children.

He amassed an enormous fortune, but when the network gave a better deal to the producers of *Happy Days*, indispensible Aaron went on a sick-out until he got more money. Like my parents, he thought he had too little.

As a Zen student, I know Buddhist monks and nuns who have nothing of their own except the robes on their backs and a set of eating utensils. One of them, who used to be a well-to-do businessman, prosperous enough to collect Shingo's paintings, is now a travelling mendicant begging for his living all over Japan, while we use the reading lamp and the antique ceramic cooking pot and the handmade soup bowls he gave us when he left ordinary life and entered a monastery.

Because of the satisfaction that comes from selflessness, and the gratification of lifting the spiritual lives of others, Zen monks and nuns feel they're among the truly wealthy. But I don't have the guts to be that rich and Shingo doesn't seem to either.

So how much is enough? I'd say it's all relative and it can be different at different times of your life.

I've shopped on Rodeo Drive and spent $1,000 on a Halston gown to wear to the Emmys (which I didn't win). I've been in a sky-high tax bracket. But, exhaustion and boredom; the knowledge that everything I "owned," house, car, the works, really belonged to a bank; and the dream-turned-drama of working in TV, exposed that lifestyle for what it was: crazy and crazy-making.

When a network executive, who'd just cancelled a project I thought I'd kill for, made the comment, "Great legs, you really wanna get this show on the air?" I understood my limitations.

"Not if I have to sleep with you, putz," I thought but didn't utter. Today, you could sue the jerk, but in those days, the term "sexual harassment" hadn't even been coined.

Shingo has lived all his adult life for art and any reasonable sum of money which comes to him from art he puts back into art. His work has been seen in museums almost from the time he left college, but, unless the museum bought the work, or at least paid all his expenses, the costs came out of his pocket. Most of the time they paid, and still do, but lack of a museum budget has never meant that he'd refuse to exhibit, even if it required shipping his work to another city or another country.

To support this unbusinesslike attitude he's been forced, on occasion, to do other work.

He's driven a truck. He's owned a recycling business in which he traded toilet paper for cast-off newspapers. He's mass-produced copies of classical paintings for a company which sold them to the public at auction in big hotels (how he hates Claude Monet and his pesky *Water Lillies*). He's even played mah-jongg for money.

All this took place when he was much younger. Some of it helped send his daughter to college. None of it allowed him to live high off the hog.

He is one of those charmed individuals, though, whose money seems to arrive just when he needs it, when his bank account is yelling, "Hey!!! Over here!!!"

He's like a guy who never goes fishing with fish in the fridge. When it's empty, he goes. Only then do the fish allow themselves to be caught.

It's been his own choice, the level of income he aimed for, but I've often marvelled that the remuneration for most fine artists should be so much smaller than what is earned by a comedy writer.

It's so because of supply and demand, size of audience, support for the medium you're working in – advertisers spend billions in support of TV – and the fact that television writers have agents, managers, and a union, The Writers' Guild of America, and artists don't.

The difference in earnings has little to do with critical praise. I made a career-high salary on *The Love Boat* which was never loved by any critic. Season after season they headlined "LOVE BOAT SINKS," or words to that effect, hoping it would. But, thanks to its true-blue audience, it sailed on.

Except for a few art-stars, the quality of art doesn't necessarily attract career-high money until after an artist dies, thereby limiting the supply of his or her unique output.

Everyone knows about Vincent van Gogh whose earnings from the one painting he sold totalled four hundred Belgian francs, which, at today's exchange rate, would equal $12.75 U.S. Now his paintings bring in seventy, eighty, and ninety million American dollars each.

Amedeo Modigliani, too, only sold a few paintings for peanuts during his short life, but his pieces now go for upwards of thirty million. I'll bet he's rolling in his grave at Pere LaChaise Cemetery.

As a television writer-producer, I had a business manager and a personal manager who took care of everything to do with money. When I went out on my own, in my mid-forties, I had to learn about finance, starting from scratch.

It alarmed me to learn that money you deposited in your bank account by check was not immediately available for use. It had a hold on it for a number of days and a check you wrote against it, which came in too soon, would bounce.

And then they charged you money to bounce it!

This was where I was starting from.

I'd never heard of a bank certificate of deposit, a CD, but soon found out that in 1984 you could earn from 9.5% to 12% on your money if you invested in them. Though that sounds like a lot today, it was much less than the 19.5% you could have earned on a one month CD, as President Jimmy Carter handed the reins to Ronald Reagan at the end of 1980.

To learn about the stock market, a knowledgeable friend suggested watching the nightly business news on TV. Though it would be confusing at first, in a few months it would begin to make sense, once you knew the difference between stocks and bonds and how to trade them, and learned the names of the companies in the news, and why they were in the news.

Reading books could also help, he said, but you'd never really understand the market until you were in it, learning from your own "Oh, boy!" successes and your own "OH, EXPLETIVE!" failures.

After a year of faithful study, I opened a brokerage account and began to trade with the help of a stock broker. Today, you can trade electronically, and do all your own research online, and I do. But even with 25 years experience, I'm still a novice.

After all, it's gambling. You have to have the stomach for it. You have to be willing to lose as well as win.

I may be the only person on Earth who lost money on Ebay: I'm still holding 100 shares and they're still lying there at two thirds of what I paid for them. I dropped $10,000, hard earned, when Worldcom went under in 2002, but I know a man who lost his house.

The Worldcom thing still bugs me, though, because, at the time, I knew an award-winning, high-earning, saleswoman who worked there. Surprisingly, she was being let go. She said Worldcom was losing money because their products weren't competitive and there was nothing new in the pipeline. But I didn't put two and two together. Who would ever have guessed that the number two phone company in the United States was getting ready to take a dive?

Living without a real job from age 45 into my sixties, when pensions kicked in, was a challenge. It required scaling down, living less expensively, and trying to obey a budget so my "principal" would last past middle age.

This was hard-headed financial planning, not a seat on the simple-living bandwagon, but it turned out to be good training for future off-grid life.

One trick, learned early, was to put every possible expense on a credit card that gives out airline miles, then pay off the balance each month so they couldn't charge interest. Why not get free travel while paying all your bills with one check?

During those years, though often a renter, I always owned a piece of property somewhere. If I wasn't living there, it was rented out, waiting for land values to increase to the point where it would make sense to sell. Real estate is one good way for the average person to make a lump sum of money, though you have to be prepared for the idiot tenant who spray-paints the bathtub navy-blue.

The goal was to own a house without having a mortgage. That way you wouldn't be indebted to a bank and in a bind if a tenant couldn't come up with the rent. Nor would you be exposed if property values dipped below the amount you'd borrowed, the reason for many a real estate mess during this recent recession.

In the late 1980's I found an inexpensive little shack on a pretty piece of land on Kauai Island and was able to pay cash for it. Fifteen years, up and down evaluations, one hurricane, and one navy-blue bathtub later, it had more than doubled in price, and its rent had paid half our rent in downtown L. A. all that time. Selling that fortunate little place allowed us to buy our off-grid home on The Big Island.

To our Zen monk friends, both Shingo and I are probably still too greedy, though most of my former show business acquaintances would view us as poor.

The Economist magazine, which rates and charts such things, often talks about "The poor," and "The Third World." They're referring to people who earn less than $1 a day; even $2 a day still qualifies you as "poor" and "Third." Incidentally, most of "the poor" live off the grid, though not necessarily by choice.

But their "poor" and our "poor" are vastly different. We're not so poor, for example, that we can't afford to give to charity. Though we are too poor to support one with large personal donations: Bill Gates will not be calling.

Our favorite charity is Heifer International, an organization aimed at the $1 and $2 a day folks.

Heifer gives livestock; not just heifers, the young cows for which it's named, but water buffalo, goats, pigs, llamas, sheep, rabbits, chickens and ducks, or bees, or trees, or seeds, along with instruction in modern farming and husbandry practices, to underfed people all over the world.

But the thing we like best is the "passing on of the gift." Whatever you get from Heifer, you must pass on some of its fruits to someone else in need. Then they do the same.

That's the thrill: each gift goes on indefinitely. Twenty dollars worth of ducks becomes an infinite number of ducks. Generations of ducks have your goodwill on them.

Another excellent ".org" is Alternative Gifts International which sponsors everything from free wheelchairs, to clean-water wells for those muddy-puddle people, to vaccines for orphans, to solar cookers for refugees.

Our way of supporting these internet-savvy charities – they have websites where you can donate by credit card – is to fundraise for them at parties. On my birthday, Shingo's birthday, or any occasion when we're inviting a bunch of guests, we put out "The Pot" for donations in lieu of gifts.

We ask each guest to throw in $1. Toward the end of the evening, someone counts the money and we all vote on who gets it.

Will we send angora rabbits, raised only for their fur, to vegetarian Nepal? Or, thinking bigger, should it be a share of a hardworking water buffalo? Wheelchairs, made from plastic garden chairs with recycled bicycle wheels, are life-changing for the people who get them. It's hard to decide how to distribute the money.

When we discover that, for another ten bucks, we could send 1,000 tree seeds to make a windbreak in the Andes of Peru, someone always comes up with it.

When we explain about passing on the gift, tens and twenties jump into The Pot.

So even the poor can help the poor.

Based on my own financial journey from ignorance to a certain understanding of wealth and what it is (not only money), I'd say that having money when you need it is certainly helpful.

I wonder how people manage without knowing how to get it and put it to work. Why don't schools teach the one subject that absolutely everyone needs to know about?

Why don't they focus on financial matters early, say in junior high, when kids start to get income from part-time jobs? Wouldn't it be good for them, and for society, if they could learn while they're young how to invest their earnings, instead of blowing them on consumer goods they'll soon tire of?

Shouldn't a capitalist country teach the next generation how to participate in capitalism?

Wouldn't teenagers flock to a course called "Money"?

If I ran the world, I'd start them in preschool.

I believe Shingo and I have enough wealth, and enough potential wealth, to provide for our remaining years off the grid in the not-inexpensive boonies, even enough to cope with an oily Saudi king. But, being a worry-wart, I still fear the unknown.

The big one: what would a prolonged illness do to us financially?

This was an issue I'd been hiding from, not addressing, not researching, just ignoring, hoping it would go away.

But it didn't. It was quietly smirking in the background, getting ready to demand my full attention.

Which it did, starting in February of 2010, when Shingo went to bed with sciatica and couldn't get up for a month.

HEALTH IN THE BOONIES

What's sciatica? A pain in the butt. Literally. Damage to a disk in your lower spine causes pain to radiate from your buttocks down your leg.

For Shingo, it came on slowly after he spent a day chain-sawing overhanging tree branches so delivery trucks could make it down our road. That night he seemed uncomfortable sitting in one place for any length of time.

It got a little worse two days later when he carried a heavy piece of furniture: I saw him limping slightly, putting more weight on his left foot than his right.

It finally nailed him when he a lifted a full propane tank, weighing 54 pounds, out of the car and began to carry it, one handed, to its final destination at the side of the house.

Carrying propane tanks was one of his standard chores, at least it had been until now, but, suddenly and forever, the lifting and shifting of a heavy metal tank of LP gas was going to be a no-no. His tailbone was telling him so. Screaming it!

He went to bed in unbearable pain, couldn't stand or walk, could barely crawl. But it took us both four days to realize that bed rest wasn't going to fix him. And no amount of massage, no hot or cold compresses, no Tiger Balm liniment, no over-the-counter pain pills were going to improve his condition. He would have to, he must, go to the hospital.

We'd been putting it off out of fear. It was going to be excruciating for him to get to the car, get into the passenger seat, live through a roller-coaster ride down our pot-holed road, make it all the way to Hilo, and then have to get out of the car again.

At the emergency waiting area in the hospital he was so doubled over that they found him a room ahead of people who'd been waiting longer.

When the doctor arrived, he was crouched on his knees on the bed with his face buried in a pillow. The doctor, whose sideline was apparently stand-up comedy, said, "Either you're in terrible pain or you're looking for your contact lenses."

The joke was lost on my husband, and not just because of the language barrier. What he came for was not yucks but morphine.

It was a smiling Shingo who exited the hospital after the injected pain killer kicked in, but he still couldn't sit down: it was either kneel or stand or lie prone, and walking was a bent-over, shuffle-along affair.

His smile, and his limited mobility, wore off along with the morphine. Once he got home, he had to count on a regime of prescribed narcotics, anti-inflammatories, and a muscle relaxant just to keep him in a holding pattern.

It was Cyclo-this and Perco-that and Predi-whatever plus mega-milligram Motrin, each of which had its own timetable for consumption: this one every four hours, that one three times a day; one should be taken with meals, another on an empty stomach.

I became the show-runner of his drugs, making an elaborate schedule and handing them out one or two at a time, worried that if he had access to all those pills at his bedside he might, intentionally or not, take more than than he should.

Seeing the pain return to his face and seeing the toll it was taking on him, imagining myself in his position, I knew I would have been tempted to over-medicate.

Meanwhile, he had to eat.

When you're "ill and ailing" as Hollywood's *Daily Variety* newspaper puts it, you really only want the food your mother made for you when you were four years old and laid up with the mumps.

In Shingo's case, that's "okayu," a plain rice gruel with only a few grains of salt added to keep it from tasting exactly like library paste. A variation on the rice and water recipe is, in fact, used to glue the paper panels onto a shoji screen.

I served it with small side dishes of pickles, or "furikake," a combination of seaweed and sesame sprinkles, blindly trusting they'd improve its blah-ness, because, as you've guessed, I never did sample it.

I thought he was starting to feel better when he asked for fish stock or chicken stock to be added to the gruel, taking it closer to a European risotto.

When he graduated to eggs for breakfast and seared tuna and a salad for dinner, I thought he was on the mend.

But we weren't out of the woods. Not yet. He still couldn't get out of bed except to limp to the bathroom with the help of a cane. He was running out of pain killers and hadn't had a full night's sleep in weeks.

To get more medicine, he was expected to see his primary care physician, who, we knew, had just left the family health center where he'd been practicing.

To our complete exasperation, it was impossible to get through to a human being at the health center by phone in order to arrange for a new primary care doctor. Leaving urgent messages did not result in a return call. Unbelievable! What to do?

As in anti-smoking days, I ransacked our medicine cabinet and came up with 6 pills of Percocet prescribed for a toothache of Shingo's in 1990. They still worked.

Then a neighbor with three of the cutest corkscrew-curly-haired children offered two more Percocet tablets left over from her home-birthing experiences. We were about to accept her offer when the miracles began to multiply.

First, a master of acupuncture and speaker of Japanese, a healer and teacher, who'd recently moved to the Big Island – I'll call him "K

58

Sensei" – drove for over an hour, out of friendship, to work on Shingo at our home.

His treatment and his explanation of what to expect from it, in English and Japanese, helped us understand that sciatica is an ailment that can be cured with conservative treatment. It can also keep you lying down for weeks or even months. He said not to hurry into everyday activities. He also offered to come back again if Shingo needed his help.

Next day, came a surprise drop-in from Suzi Gillette, the real estate broker from Kauai who'd helped us buy our off-grid home. She happened to be coming from the office of a doctor who worked up and down the coast of East Hawaii out of a mobile home. "You should call him," she said.

Almost with my next breath, I did, and may have seemed too overjoyed when he personally answered the phone.

I made an appointment for us to go and meet him, explaining Shingo's no-primary-care situation. He said, "No problem," he'd be in our area in a couple of days.

We met in a parking lot, like spies having a clandestine rendezvous – except how clandestine can you be in the parking lot of a church? The doctor, a young M.D., was able to re-prescribe Shingo's pills, to our obvious relief.

He'd also studied Eastern medicine and practiced a style of acupuncture in which the needles are connected to an electric current. He thought it could be of help, but, because it would be too hard for Shingo to make it up the stairs into his mobile home/office, the doctor treated him while he was lying face down on the flattened front seat of our car, with the door left open and Shingo's bottom, rap-star style, partially exposed. After inserting his acupuncture needles, the Doc connected him by extension cord to a portable battery!

As it turned out, this creative M.D. lived only a few minutes from our home, so he later offered to make two housecalls, giving Shingo more acupuncture, and some massage, helping to ease him off his medications. It was never again necessary to renew the prescriptions.

During this time we couldn't make it to potlucks down the street. So the entire potluck crowd, nine in all, came to us, bringing Shingo little gifts and homemade desserts, making a fuss over him, letting him know he was loved.

But my poor husband: four weeks in, and he was still spending most of his time in bed. The most amazing miracle was the one that got him on his feet again.

It's a Chinese herb called Dong Chong Xia Cao, mailed to him by K Sensei, who told him it would get him up in two days with no more pain.

It got him up in one!

But there's more to the story: the Chinese name Dong Chong Xia Cao means Winter Worm Summer Plant. The herb that did the trick starts out in the high Himalayas of Tibet when a giant moth lays an egg on the ground. The egg grows into a larva, which buries itself in the soil, where it's attacked and consumed by a fungus, which then shoots up out of the earth as a plant. Who on earth would ever dream of eating such a thing?

We found out, by accident, months later, when viewing a BBC TV series called *Wild China,* from Netflix.

We watched the plant coming out of the ground and learned that Tibetan herders, 1,000 years ago, noticed that their yaks had more energy after eating it, so they decided to give it try. To be frank about it, the yaks were more sexually active. The herders were gobbling yak Viagra.

This rare herb turned out to have many healing properties and was subsequently reserved for the nobility and hoarded like gold for centuries in Asia. Today it's synthesized in California and you can get it over the internet. It comes by mail in a few days. That's two more miracles, right there.

But now to cost. Having been through this episode of illness, albeit nothing life-threatening, and nothing chronic (cross your fingers), cost is the last thing you think about when someone you love is hurting.

But there are going to be expenditures.

This time, the hospital bill was covered by Medicare and drug costs were nothing to complain about considering their brief role in his recovery.

The mobile doctor didn't accept insurance. No wonder: they take forever to pay and the paperwork is too time consuming. So we paid for his services in cash. His requested fee was too low, we felt, in view of our gratitude for his contribution to Shingo's recovery. We insisted he take more money.

Considering that K Sensei, and his powers of healing, are beyond ordinary remuneration, we asked his wife to choose a framed piece of Shingo's art for their new home.

As for Winter Worm Summer Plant, Dong Chong Xia Cao, we continue to buy it on the net at $29.95 for 100 capsules and Shingo uses it as a tonic at the least suggestion of sciatica. He also does a strengthening exercise shown him by an artist friend. An accomplished massage therapist in Hilo pointed out that one of his legs is shorter than the other: adjusting his posture will help him to avoid problems. He also uses a bamboo charcoal mat to increase his body temperature and circulation in bed at night: it's one of those little-known Japanese health aids that those who've discovered it swear by.

All in all, with the exception of the emergency hospital interlude, you might describe the management of Shingo's sciatica as "off-grid health care."

But let's not negate that hospital treatment, which he couldn't have done without. That it was paid for by Medicare, the U. S. Government's automatic insurance program for people over 65, seemed like a miracle, too.

How to insure its citizens' good health is such a divisive political issue in the United States. It's impossible to pass a law about it without making half the country mad.

That surprises us because both Canada and Japan, our native countries, have universal insurance coverage and nobody thinks twice about it.

I used to be insured by a Writers' Guild medical plan paid for by my various employers, but when I took early retirement I discovered, to my chagrin, that I'd have to self-pay. If I'd worked for two more years, I'd have been covered for life for free.

Being horribly healthy, I never did self-pay. I chose to look upon the lack of insurance as an inducement.

Having no coverage from age 45 to 65, when Medicare kicked in, meant I had to be aware and take good care, eating well, practicing meditation and yoga, working out with weights, walking, swimming, roller-skating, skiing. It also meant I saved about $36,000.

Luckily, there were no hospital expenses, and some dental work was done in exchange for Shingo's art, but the rest of the regular and emergency doctor and dentist appointments were paid out of pocket. Those never exceeded $700 a year, so I still saved at least $22,000.

This way of approaching things was a lot like playing the stock market. You could lose and lose big. But, honestly, I felt that buying health insurance was betting against myself.

My mother, a Canadian, had government health insurance, which, in my opinion, hastened her death.

She lived in St. Catharines, Ontario, which caters to senior citizens with a hospital on every other block, and so many MRI machines you'd almost wish you had a disease so you could go and find out what it is.

The instant accessibility of Western medicine had her seeing doctors for every little thing. And they prescribed a drug for every little thing. And every new drug had a new side effect. By the time she was my age, her stomach was a wreck, her general health had disintegrated, and the drugs no longer worked.

One of her doctors recommended that she be operated on for an aneurism at age 74. When I asked him "Would you do this operation on your own mother?" he said, "That's not a fair question."

As they were about to wheel her down the hall for the procedure, another doctor entered her hospital room and said, "Of course, we're just going to take care of the one aneurism. To get the other one we'd have had to send her to Toronto."

She died three days later.

I've always wondered, would that operation have been performed without the certainty of a government payout? How necessary was it, if they were going to leave her with another aneurism?

Fortunately, we've lived in an era when there are complements and alternatives to the health care my mother depended on. Psychotherapy, nutritional therapy, lifestyle change, yoga, acupuncture, Alexander Technique, chiropractic, massage, visualization, herbal medicine, vitamin supplements, and, most useful of all, meditation, are some of the preventive and healing methods I've used with success in my own life.

And then there are the offbeat and even slightly loony folk remedies which always appear under the title, "What Your Doctor Doesn't Want You To Know."

Recently, I heard about a recipe made with raisins soaked in gin. It's supposed to ward off all kinds of old-age aches and pains, so, sure, I gave it a try.

You soak a pound of golden raisins in a glass jar of good gin and wait until the raisins absorb the alcohol. You then consume precisely 8 raisins a day.

I'm not sure it does all it's cracked up to do, but I like the sweetly ginny jolt I get when I take it around four o'clock in the afternoon, and so continue with the recommended dose, sometimes even sneaking in an extra raisin.

But faced with the kind of sciatic pain Shingo endured, a lovely Western pain-killing drug goes right to the top of my list. A newly minted antibiotic sometimes comes in handy, too. Two friends have survived cancer death-sentences with individually tailored chemotherapy, so I'd never say "never."

Shingo was finally out of bed but he couldn't do anything. He couldn't stand at the sink and do dishes, yet, although he tried. He couldn't fill five gallon jugs, four at a time, in the town of Keaau, with drinking water, then lift them into the car and out again and into the house and up onto the water cooler. He couldn't carry five gallon containers of generator gas, or haul the heavy laundry to the laundromat, and he certainly couldn't drag around the spine-destroying propane tanks.

While he was laid up, I'd already added these chores to my routine of cooking three meals a day, cleaning up, grocery shopping in Hilo, picking up mail at the post office, taking garbage to the dump, and fireplace management, but now it looked as though these extra jobs might become my permanent responsibility. For that to work without harming my own health, some re-thinking had to happen.

There must be no more five gallons of gas. Too heavy. Three gallons is all I can lift comfortably, so I only partially filled the cans. How hard was that?

For the drinking water, I balked at going to Keaau to the water machine, filling bottles every month. I decided to boil our own catchment water and fill the five gallon bottles to a three gallon level.

This took up time and space in the kitchen and wasn't the best way to solve the problem. But Shingo did, later, when he researched, bought, and installed a new water filter on the kitchen sink. It purified and made our catchment water potable. Ha!!!

Laundry could be done by others at the laundromat. I took advantage of this service and asked the ladies to give me smaller bundles of fluff-and-fold so I could carry them to the car and into the house without strain.

That just left the dreaded propane tanks to deal with.

But this is the Island of Hawaii, right? This is East Hawaii. This, in fact, is Puna, which means "life-giving waters," the outrageously beautiful, if sometimes damp, not to say soaking wet, district where the essence of aloha lives large.

This is a place where the kid who filled the propane at Hirano's General Store took one look at us, judged our auntie and uncle age, and lifted the tanks into our car, whether he was a boy or one of several twenty-something girls. They'd pick them up and slide them into the trunk, even though there was a sign hanging over the filling station which stated clearly that they were not required to do this extra work. They did it out of kindness, out of gentleness, with the most charming of smiles.

When we got the tanks home, I could slide them out of the trunk and maneuver them, using a handcart, to where they needed to be. I didn't want to let Shingo touch them. His sciatic nerve was more important.

In time, he was back doing dishes. (Did I mention he was raised in a restaurant? He's programmed to clean up.)

He was back doing laundry, and we'd take turns on trips to the dump.

He was, again, the guy who drove us everywhere, even though driving did tire his back.

He was also still the only one who knew how to re-start the on-demand hot water heater and the propane refrigerator when they had their occasional hissy-fits.

He fixed the toilet when the who-jigee that lifts the whatchamacallit to make the water flush, quit.

He, once again, got on the roof and cleaned out gutters. He even decided to scrape any remaining paint blisters off the house and re-prime and re-paint.

This was our new normal. But later, when we get really old, who knows?

I can't lose sleep over it though. As predicted by generations of Zen masters, and as proven here in Paradise, although things are sure to change, if you let them, they have a way of working out.

FASHION & BEAUTY, SORT OF

"I've just turned seventy," I tell someone.

"You don't look it," they reply.

This makes me feel young and beautiful until I recall that I've always said such things to much older women, even if they were crones.

"I like your outfit," a woman says, and I'm tempted to feel fashionable until I remember that every woman always says such things to every other woman. It's like dogs sniffing each other, a ritual greeting.

Fashion and beauty, beauty and fashion: it's flogged to us day and night, on TV, in newspapers, magazines, and on the internet. No matter what your age, there's a product or an item of apparel sure to make you more appealing.

It's the latest. It's a must-have. It'll make you hipper and hotter. You'll look like a movie star who's spent thousands on plastic surgery. It'll give you whiter teeth, fewer wrinkles, longer eyelashes, better hair, or, if yours is falling out, it'll put some back.

You'll teeter on strappy spike heels borrowed from the wardrobe of a dominatrix. Your handbag will be so huge you could put all your groceries in it. And you'd better buy those new pants in at least three sizes because of all the weight you're going lose with the "No surgery! No exercise required! Pounds melt away!" diet pills.

I can't say I'm past any interest in beauty products. I do want fewer wrinkles and whiter teeth and lots of healthy hair, but I have my own routes to these results, though they're not exactly trending.

I've stopped shampooing: no more soapy stuff, no more revitalizing treatments, no more leave-ins, no more shaping gel. I just massage an aloe cream into my scalp, rinse it out, then blow-dry. It works for keeping hair on your head and not in your hairbrush, it eliminates all those time-consuming and expensive products, and the results, to me, are just as good or better.

The same aloe cream is my everyday moisturer, and for whiter teeth it's peroxide in water, swished, and/or baking soda on a toothbrush.

I have one hair confession, though: adding blonde streaks to a deadly-drab hair color has been a lifelong habit and I'm still doing it. Like my mother, though more than eligible, I'm not turning gray. Too bad. It would save a lot of time and trouble.

I do love clothes. I love fashion. When, in my early twenties, I lived in Toronto, my upstairs neighbor and landlord was designer David Smith, known as "the father of boutiques in Toronto." For a birthday present he made me a dress with the first micro-mini skirt ever seen in that city.

When I wore it, on a lovely spring day, for a walk down Yonge Street, a busy thoroughfare, a middle-aged British gentleman in a dark green Jaguar Mark Seven sedan braked suddenly, rolled down his window and yelled, "LOWER YOUR SKIRT!!!"

Those revealing skirts are back now, but I'm not wearing them. I don't want to scare anybody. I'm leaving them to you my young long-legged friend.

I'm also leaving to you the colorful "mod" clothes we wore in the sixties, the midi-skirts and long coats of the seventies, the never-out-of-my-jeans but how about this silk shirt and the label on my designer jacket? look of the eighties.

I'm leaving to you all enslavement to what's in and what's out, what's old and what's new, because nothing is. It's all been done and will be done again. If we wait long enough, they'll bring back bustles.

So as much as I love fashion, I love it most, these days, on someone else. Someone in a magazine which I'm free-reading at the check-out stand in the supermarket. Someone who just spent a fortune on her *haute couture* outfit though it may not be entirely becoming on her. Someone who's dressed to kill but photographed from a top-down angle which gives the fashion-plate a big head, skinny legs, knobby knees, and strangely large feet.

At all the New York charity and fashion events, they must squeeze all the photographers into a shooting gallery which guarantees these unattractive outcomes: you see so many of them when free-reading.

The fashions I love best these days are seen not in a magazine but in our back yard, and the wearer is not a person but a bird.

The toniest of these is a wild rooster who's decided to show up once in a while to wow us with his sartorial elegance. He's so splendid that I've swallowed all my anti-rooster, anti-chicken opinions. He's a Moa, a Red Junglefowl. Shingo calls him "Jack."

His sleek curved black tail with emerald green metallic undertones adorns a muscular bronze and turquoise feathered body. His blood-red head-comb and wattle accessorize his nattiness to perfection.

And his poses: his poses would put a runway model doing the Paris collections to shame. My favorite is his "I'm a weathervane" side-view, when he perches on a fence with his head and tail held high, then stretches into full cock-a-doodle-doo bearing just before he flaps his wings and lets go with a "Check out my sexy self!" full throated cry. Thank goodness he's only a rent-a-rooster: he really is loud.

His wife, or significant other, whom we've named "Betty" – after the unread "Jack and Betty" English text-book of Shingo's youth – and her baby chick, also occasional visitors, are not as well dressed. Mum is comparatively frumpy in her brown feathers, and the chick, whom we've named "Yolanda" for no good reason, is turning from a creamy butter-ball to mother-and-daughter matching brown.

Also jungle fowl, they're self sufficient. They can find their own food – though Shingo just has to feed them – and they sleep in trees.

They have an illustrious island history having arrived with the original Hawaii Island settlers, Polynesian ocean voyagers, who brought them here to raise for food.

Perhaps, like some pedigree'd upper-crust women, these females have no interest in, even a distain for, flashy fashions. Regardless, it's fun to watch them come and go and realize that phrases, used over the years, like "under her wing," or "ruffled her feathers" are based on observations of a real hen and chick.

Betty's close attention to baby Yolanda gives her the aura of beauty that surrounds every new mother, and Yolanda's antics as she learns to run fast, and fly, and catch worms and skinks, are naively beautiful, too.

Or perhaps we're just glowing over the semi-fulfillment of Shingo's chicken dreams: his "they're just visiting," no-mites-on-us, left-handed way of having poultry sauntering around.

Next-best dressed would be the opera singer in our forest, "Melodious Laughing Thrush," a copper-colored songbird with a slender creamy outline of feathers around its eyes which resemble the retro cat's-eye white-framed glasses now coming back into vogue.

This bird clearly has good taste but no self-confidence. It can't stop looking in a mirror. With no actual mirrors in the wilderness, it substitutes our car windshield, the sliding door to Shingo's studio, a window in my office, even the solar panels on the roof, which it peers at and pecks at, sometimes dangling off a fern frond to get access to its reflection. Either Melodious is overly concerned with its looks, or it thinks the bird in the mirror is a potential Mrs. Melodious.

Also stylish are the red-feathered cardinals flashing through the forest. Luckily for them, they're not the envied birds whose feathers were plucked to make the full-length feather-work capes of fashionable Hawaiian royalty in centuries gone by.

I used to think those birds were killed for their feathers, but I've learned that only three feathers could be taken from any one bird, which was then released, and that, therefore, the iconic red and yellow royal feathered capes and head-dresses took more than one generation to make.

One traditional Hawaiian fashion statement that's never gone away is the wearing of flowers, the fabulously fragrant ginger, gardenia, plumeria, pua kenikeni, jasmine, and endless varieties of orchids, worn as leis, or behind the ear, or in the hair, or on a hatband, not just by women but by men.

There's a story about a Hawaiian paniolo cowboy who entered a mainland rodeo and won all his events, raising the question, "Who's the bronco buster with the flowers on his hat?"

Flowers too big or too heavy to be worn, like hibiscus, anthuriums, or heliconias, become the subject of flamboyant Hawaiian fabric designs for casual shirts, board shorts, muumuus, and sarongs. Surfers, hula dancers, people using walkers, businessmen and babies, all sport these brightly colored costumes in the islands.

But Shingo and I are not among them. He's colorful enough in his paint-spattered sweat pants and tops. For dress-up, it's the orange fleece Polo shirt given to him by another artist in Los Angeles ten years ago. There, he was known as "orange man" it was so much a part of his uniform. He's still often in it.

For temple duties it's a black kimono with an ochre-colored one-shoulder robe which echos the robe of the Buddha; or the pale blue cotton work clothes known as "samu-e," the looks-good-on-everyone outfit he was wearing the day I met him.

Shingo's low blood pressure keeps him colder than most people. Add the fact that we live in a mountain environment and he's always bundled up.

You've heard of the musical group "The Four Tops"? Their name describes the three layers of tee-shirts he's wearing under whatever else he's wearing.

Long-johns go over his Jockeys, too. And that's in summer. Then layer after layer comes off as we descend the mountain into Hilo where it's much warmer than at our house. If there's a bathing suit under all those layers, he's equipped for one more Big Island occasion.

He's also wearing rubber boots – a lot – in places where rubber boots aren't particularly necessary. Like Hilo, which has pavement wherever you need it.

This is a big twist on his former city-dweller image. In college days in Tokyo, the wearing of rubber boots suggested the country bumpkin. "Rubber boot boy" was a slur, embarrassing to someone whose childhood home, Nagaoka, in Northern Japan, which also had all the pavement you could ever want, was surrounded by rice fields. His name, "Honda," means "ricefield owner," read "farmer."

But the wearing of rubber boots may have less to do with his ancestral occupation, and more to do with his given name, "Shingo," which means "truly myself." It may just be a pointed statement of a newfound independence from public opinion.

Though I'm not especially anti-color, I like to wear black. It's the lazy-woman's way to look relatively pulled together: black shoes, black pants, black shirt, and you never have to change your black handbag. It's easy to accessorize with simple jewellery, a colorful scarf, or any lovely lei.

As a top, I like a turtleneck. It can have long sleeves or none, as long as it's got that special feature. I'm borrowing the look from Kathryn Hepburn in her old age. Remember how her turtlenecks turned into hoods as she hid more and more of her neck?

That's my reason, too. Without a costly nip and tuck, all necks get scrawnier and chins get jowlier with age. But, under a turtleneck, who needs to know?

If anyone in Hilo, or other hotspots, comments that I seem warmly dressed, I explain that I'm on my way to the supermarket, which, everyone understands, is a place where you could freeze to death from air-conditioning while they try to keep their frozen foods frozen and their fresh produce fresh.

I used to have a landlady in Hollywood who, in her seventies, had platinum blonde hair and wore splashy Pucci knockoff dresses, loads of clanky costume jewellery, and, her fashion signature, clear plastic Spring-o-lator mules with rhinestone heels. The Spring-o-lator shoe had come and gone with the fifties, and I swore at the time, never to betray my over-the-hillness by wearing such outdated footgear when I reached her age. But I am.

My version of the Spring-o-lator is a 1990's Steve Madden high-rise platform slip-on – black, of course – which adds an inch and a half to my 5'-5" height. You know this shoe: it has a heavy composition rubber sole with an elasticized upper. It's been out of style for eons and isn't showing any sign of returning to buzzworthy but I'm still a fan: it's so comfortable. I own two pairs and they're not wearing out, but if they did I'd take them to the shoemaker and get them stitched, glued, or lasered back together until there was no further hope. Because not only are they comfortable, I don't want to be short.

I wasn't planning to be wide, either, but it's becoming a distinct possibility since we quit smoking. I'm gaining weight. Shingo's not.

I'm putting food in my mouth instead of a cigarette. He's not. But one good thing about adding a few pounds is that it does plump out your wrinkles.

The ancient Hawaiian ideal of beauty is a woman we'd now call obese. The old Hawaiian queens were so gigantic, they needed the help of more than one person to stand up when they were seated or lying down. To be thin meant to be deprived. To be robust and over-flowing provided a symbol of abundance to the people.

Some vestige of this way of thinking still exists in Hawaii. Clothing buyers stint on the small sizes and over-order on the large, extra large, and extra-extra-read-all-about-it.

Mainland girls have been harangued for so long with negative stories about overweight and supermodel-thin examples of how you should look, that some young women – including supermodels – starve themselves, do drugs, or become bulemic, yorking up their dinners, to maintain an unnatural skinniness.

Here, that's not happening. Big is still better. Big on a woman still attracts the perfect man: the wide shouldered, slim hipped, athletic boy who will mate with the girl who looks most like his mother.

He'll be the gorgeous guy I see in stores with his baby boy in the cart and his little girl running alongside. He'll be the beautiful dad he wants to be. And his wife, size large, walking next to him, will have a winning smile on her face.

Her smile, that stunning Hilo display of exultation which says, "Isn't life wonderful?!" is a thing that's missing from *Vogue Magazine*. It's missing from the runways in Rome, Paris, and New York, which claim to have a corner on fashion and beauty. But, trust me, they don't.

East Hawaii has the corner on it, in the person of a crossing guard at the public school in Mountain View. She's certainly fifty plus, with waist-length graying hula dancer's hair, sparkling eyes, a yellow hard-hat, and a day-glo orange safety jacket. Her smile lights up a rainy day and she showers it on everyone who passes. You can't drive by without feeling somehow subtly healed.

Another top model is a county traffic controller, well padded, mid-twenties, who stands with a STOP sign at tree trimming sites along the highway. She's there for hours doing a repetitive job, but you never see a frown on her. She has a smile for everyone she stops and then lets go. I can't describe her clothes for the "fashion" side of this report because her attitude outweighs their importance. I doubt if anyone notices what she's wearing, but they're sure to remember her aloha.

Though most of the clothing seen at our house may best be described as "vintage," it has a certain understated luxury. It's the luxury of not having to fret too much about what you're going to put on. Since you've been wearing it for twenty years, you know what it looks like.

As for my own vanity and occasional preoccupation with wrinkles, one thing I've learned in East Hawaii: a smile is the best facelift.

INFIDELITY, KIND OF

Besides fashion and beauty, a best-selling topic of magazines at the supermarket check-out is infidelity. To know this, you don't even have to free-read, just scan the glossy covers to see who's messing around on whom. Is your favorite movie star the tear-stained jilted beauty or the other woman? From time to time the same actress may be playing either role.

Such things do happen in real life, too, by which I mean the lives of people who aren't famous, even though they may live in Hollywood.

One friend, there, lost her husband to a porn extra. Not a porn star, a porn *extra*. How would that make you feel?

Another friend, a shapely African-American former Playboy Bunny, lost hers to an aging Polish poetess who walked with a cane.

Yet another, a beautiful Nordic blond, lost hers to a clown named Queeny.

There's no accounting for tastes, no matter where you live. But I've never heard of someone losing their husband to a chicken.

At least not until now.

That someone is me. The husband is Shingo. The chicken is Yolanda The Usurper. He's in love!

"Yolanda, Yolanda!" he cries, jumping out of bed first thing in the morning. Abandoning warmth and comfort, abandoning me, he rushes to dress and carry chicken feed outside, scattering it near the old ohia tree, in front of the smiling tiki sculpture made for us by Felix Niihau.

74

"Yolanda, Yolanda!" he calls her name again and again until she arrives and starts pecking away.

As you know, we first met Yolanda when she was a few days old, visiting our place with her mother, Betty. She was a tiny pale-yellow fluff-ball then, an only child, which caused much neighborhood comment:

"Only one? What happened to the rest of them?"

We couldn't say.

Let me repeat: these are wild chickens.

They don't live here. We don't know where they came from. We don't know where they go.

We're not their owners, just observers, watching Yolanda learn from Betty how to run and climb and fly and feed and groom herself.

Sure, it's endearing, and yes, we've disobeyed our chicken-raising friends by naming them. But we vowed to remain aloof, not to become too emotionally involved, as the darling little chickie-poo, Yolanda, grew into the ugliest pre-teen pullet you've ever seen.

Like a twelve year old girl with zits and braces, she went through her legs-too-long, head-too-small, have-hysteria-over-nothing stages, still watched over and protected by Betty, though much too big, now, to fit under her wing.

One morning she was screeching and clucking, at least forty feet high in an ohia tree, scared stiff, clutching the branch she was on, with Mom below, yelling at her to "Fly! Fly down, already!", which she finally did.

From that moment, she was fully able to take care of herself. She could sleep in the trees and fly down in the morning. She'd be safe from Hawaii's predators. She could eat naturally occuring seeds, bugs, worms, whatever was being served by nature – or by Shingo.

But soon after her X-treme survival demonstration, Betty turned on her, shrieking and biting and kicking her away. She was no longer allowed to follow Betty everywhere she went.

Yolanda was literally kicked out of the nest, forced to be on her own. It was sad to watch her being rebuffed, even though we understood the logic of it.

A few days after that, Betty disappeared. Yolanda was left behind to wander, disconsolate, around our back yard. That's when she stole Shingo's heart.

He can strongly identify with an abandoned child, having been one himself.

When he was ten years old, his gorgeous mother went out for a loaf of bread and never came back. He still remembers her wearing an elaborate kimono and cloak, overdressed to go grocery shopping, leaving the restaurant his father owned in Nagaoka on a snowy winter day, in her high traditional wooden shoes, patting him as he played in the snow, and she passed by.

They met again and reconciled in Tokyo many years later, but the pain of that moment will never go away. I'm sure it's one reason why he's so overly solicitous of Yolanda, never letting her out of his sight, sometimes feeding her three times a day.

But there's also another reason: he recently revealed that he'd tried to raise chickens more than once as a boy and they always died.

The lightbulb in the incubator box went out and they succumbed to the cold; or they disappeared overnight – keeping a cat and trying to raise chickens don't necessarily go together.

Since that time, he says, he's felt like a chicken's worst enemy.

The first year we lived in Hawaii he tried again to raise chickens with no success.

He built a coop and adopted two broody hens sitting on fourteen eggs in a basket, but had to return them, after only a few days, to the friend who gave them to us, when we both were gorged upon by the afore-mentioned bird-mites.

When Betty appeared with her chick he believed he was being given another chance.

And because Betty was a Hawaiian legend who could manage on her own, living free, without a coop and all its paraphernalia, not staying in one place gathering mites, he could enjoy their company almost as a bystander, without any real responsibility.

But with Betty gone there was only Yolanda.

He was down to his last chicken.

He was also quite sure Betty was dead. And depressed about it.

But I assured him she was probably sitting on eggs somewhere nearby.

Why would I think that? Because friends with poultry say that when hens sit on eggs they absolutely refuse to move. They won't eat and only leave their nests for brief periods to go to the powder room. In short, they're too busy to come visiting.

But after more than two weeks with no sign of Betty, I began to lose faith. I was starting to worry and I hadn't even seen the mongoose, yet.

You know about mongooses, right? They were brought here in 1883 as a biological control to prey on destructive, dangerous rats which were arriving by ship from all over the world and damaging economically important sugarcane.

Mongooses (mongeese?) look like low-slung squirrels with skimpy tails – picture a mink in a cheap fur coat. They're speedy things that can dart out of the forest, outracing even an onrushing car, to grab their prey with sharp slashing teeth.

Unfortunately, they have yet to get their teeth on a rat because the rat works at night and the mongoose hunts by day, so Ratty and Rikki-Tikki-Tavi never meet. (Thank you, scientists, for your in-depth research! You've done a wonderful job!)

Instead, the mongoose eats the eggs of ground-nesting Hawaiian birds, like the state mascot, "Nene", the Hawaiian goose; and the Hawaiian duck; the Hawaiian stilt; the Hawaiian coot; the Hawaiian moorhen; and the birds themselves, taking them from "rare" to "endangered." They also prey on wild and domesticated chickens, eating their eggs and young.

Having no natural enemies but plenty of chow, including fruit, frogs, lizards, crabs, and baby turtles, the mongoose population exploded and is unstoppable.

Rats, unstoppable too, also eat all the same things, and gnaw through plastic, cardboard, wood, metal screening, and fiberglass insulation to get at them, meanwhile harming the human population with rat-lung disease, which can put you in a coma and/or kill you; and leptospirosis, which merely attacks your liver and kidneys.

We have rats at our house despite an ongoing campaign against them. Though they're absolutely not welcome, they are very talented.

I saw one, formerly employed, no doubt, by Cirque Du Soleil, climb up a fern tree, scamper out to the very end of a frond, bounce there a few times, then fly into one of our bird feeders which is five feet off the ground and usually inaccessible except to those with wings.

But all rats must go. Mice, too.

Since mongoose hours of operation don't affect them, we use a battery powered rodent trap called The Rap Zapper, sort of a rat electric chair, which electrocutes them, supposedly humanely. This eliminates the need for cat ownership and the pageant when your pet brings you the gift of a half-eaten dead rat and deposits it in your bed.

We just have to remember to check the trap. One thing you don't want is a rat that's been in there a month and has lost its composure, i.e. decomposed.

But I'm getting away from my story . . .

It was more than three weeks after she'd disappeared when I looked out the window and saw Betty. There she was next to Felix's smiling tiki trying to keep her wings around six, SIX!, "Shingo, Shingo come and see! It's Betty with SIX LITTLE BABIES!"

Her chicks couldn't have been more than a day or two old, they were hardly bigger than the eggs they came from.

At this point, both of us fell head over heels with the wonderful little eggs-with-wings which Betty had hatched out in the woods and now started bringing over for lunch, and maybe breakfast or dinner, according to her whim. Love and concern for Mama Betty escalated accordingly.

But apparently Jack, our now-and-then rooster, her old lover, and Yolanda's father, was not 100% the Dad. It seemed all too obvious when you observed that three of her chicks looked just like Yolanda, a mix of Jack plus Betty, but the other three were coffee-brown, or black and white.

78

"Yeah," said our neighbor Ranger Rita, regarding Betty's lack of constancy, "She definitely crossed the tracks."

It was two days after Betty's return when I saw a mongoose race across the road about 500 yards ahead of our place: a rare occurance and an unwanted one.

Right away, we both became over-protective of Betty's kids. So much for "no responsibility for the completely self-sufficient legendary chickens." Every time Betty and her brood veered toward the mongoose side of our property, we'd be right there yelling, "No! No! Betty! Danger!" Even though there's no telling where that mongoose went. It could be miles from here. It could be anywhere. And we haven't seen it since.

Meanwhile, Shingo was concerned about Yolanda, who was being dive-bombed by her mother whenever she came within ten yards of the new six-pack. Yolanda wanted to join the scampering chicks as they followed after Betty but she wasn't having it.

Shingo decided to feed them at separate times to make sure Betty and Yolanda didn't have a dust-up. All this rejection by her mother, he felt, was sure to affect Yolanda's self esteem so he bent over backwards to take care of her.

Absurd, isn't it, how we project our personal stories onto animals and make them stand-ins for ourselves? Aren't they just living their lives parallel to ours, not really acting out the soap operas we dream up for them?

I wonder if they know we're loading our loves and hates and hopes and fears and all our traumas, in Jungian fashion, onto the shoulders of every bird and beast in the forest.

I wonder if they know we've written tall tales about them, making them act and speak like us, as Bambi, and Bugs, and Big Bird, and Kermit, and Mickey, and Rikki-Tikki-Tavi?

Lately, Shingo has been identifying with Betty's #6, the chick who won't conform. This little fellow, or girl, we don't know yet, strays away from its family, off in its own world, then has to run like mad to catch up with them whenever they move on.

This reminds Shingo of being the next-to-last child in his own large family. Once, at a tender age, on a trip to a local festival, he got lost and his parents and siblings didn't notice until he found them again. They wondered why he was crying his eyes out.

Now, in his sixty-sixth year, with psychotherapy from #6, he realizes he was the one who wandered off and has been wandering off ever since.

Also, lately, he's been connecting Yolanda's name with mine. He says it's because we're both only-children, but there's a more insulting reason, I believe: Yolanda's hysteria. Facing any imagined threat, she panics and runs around like the well known chicken with its head cut off.

This, unfortunately, describes me to a tee. And, after twenty-some-odd years, Shingo knows it, and I can't deny it. But don't you agree it's insensitive and ungallant, not to say downright rude of him, to poke fun at my wimpishness so pointedly?

All this chicken to-do has taken place within the last year, but it's given us so many laughs and so much pleasure.

"You cannot buy this kind happiness," Shingo said, patting his heart, as we watched Betty gather up her brood and sit on them.

Then, two days later, she and the six were gone. It's just us and Yolanda now. We have no idea where they went.

Was it lack of loyalty or infidelity that made her go? Probably not. Just legendary chicken business-as-usual.

But we really miss her. Like forsaken lovers, we're constantly watching, listening for chick peeps, longing for Betty's return.

And now, with Yolanda having a bigger claim than ever on Shingo's affections, he's completely at her beck and call.

I have a hen-pecked husband.

HOW SOON THEY FORGET

Some friends came over for lunch the other day and one of them was wracking her brain for a tidbit of information which downright refused to reveal itself. She tapped her head and commented, "My memory's so bad. I'm getting old."

She's not *getting* old. She's ninety-three. But I challenged her notion, one shared by most of us, that we'll be more and more forgetful with age.

I asked another guest if he ever lost track of his main thought, or couldn't spit out the answer to a question, or couldn't remember someone's name. He said it often happened to him. He's eleven.

Likewise, it's often happened to me. Most embarrassing, and therefore never-to-be-forgotten, though it dates back to the 1960's: at a party for a close friend's engagement, I blanked on her name while trying to toast the future bride. "Here's to uh ...uh . . ."

From time to time, I've forgotten my zip code, social security number, even my own phone number, long before I was old.

A friend on Oahu recently complained about her failing memory. She was supposed to bring a file of information to a doctor's appointment for her husband. She set out the file and reminded herself more than once to bring it. And yet she forgot.

She was shocked that she forgot. She couldn't believe she forgot. The file was waiting by the front door. But she forgot to bring it.

She said she thought her mind was going. But I have a different take on it and told her so.

Like me, she used to work in Hollywood and on location, under incredible pressure. She had to remember a thousand things each day. If she forgot, the show could not go on.

But now, what takes up much of her time is to gaze at the many moods of Kaneohe Bay, just as I gaze at the beauty of the Big Island rainforest. We've forgotten what pressure is, thank goodness. But it means that we don't always bring the file.

Nowadays, it seems, there are more things than ever for people to remember. Just trying to recall the user-names and passwords for online accounts at e-mail providers, Amazon, Netflix, and all the other places we do business, is too much.

Trying to keep this muddle in mind, even if it were possible, could lead to mental meltdown, so I've removed it from my brain and put it in a binder which is already full to overflowing. Old fashioned, huh? Writing stuff down?

Last night, while tooth-brushing before bed, I found myself blurting "Edith Piaf!" through minty foam. It's the answer to 54 Across in yesterday's crossword puzzle which I'd been trying to come up with all day.

"*La Vie En Rose* singer" was the clue. How on-the-nose easy is that?

But doesn't it so often happen that the information you're chasing comes to you only after you've stopped thinking about it?

I'm used to this. I refuse to see long time lags, or instances when the answer never does come, as signs of senility. It's just the couch-potato memory I've always had.

I've even tried to train it, but with unplanned outcomes.

At MTM on *The Bob Newhart Show* we often worked with director Jay Sandrich, whose name I could never remember. He was widely known and well liked and deserved better, so I tried a word association method to imprint his name on my memory.

"Jay": a jay is a blue bird. And "Sandrich" sounds like sandwich.

Stuck in my head from then on were the prompt words "Bluebird Sandwich," and that's how I think of him to this day.

Three Weeks To A Better Memory, a book by Brendan Byrne, promises "wealth, popularity, happiness, success and personal power" if I will only use his "new, unique method for just 15 minutes a day for 21 days" to sharpen my memory.

I'm putting all this in the present tense, though the book has been on my shelf for, oh, maybe about the same length of time as *Allan Carr's Easyway to Quit Smoking*. Never have opened the cover, but there's always the possibility. It's right there at my fingertips, so, you never know, maybe I'll finally use his "simple, scientific, foolproof way to win admiration, friendship and success through" . . . uh . . . uh . . . what was it?

Shingo's memory can't be qualified or quantified since he's thinking and speaking and writing in two very different languages – make that three: English, Japanese, and Shinglish – which is enough to scramble anyone's cerebral cortex.

If he's been reading a Japanese novel or speaking to Japanese friends I need to be aware that his mind is tuned to his native tongue and that I may have to repeat myself several times in mine before he changes the dial. Even then I may hear the phrase, "What meaning?" relating to something I think he knows quite well.

Usually we depend on his hand-held Japanese/English translating computer to clarify a "Huh?", but sometimes, particularly with medical or technical terms, the machine's not up to the task. In that case, we Google, but a detailed explanation in English may bring us right back to "What meaning?"

He works hard at pronouncing and remembering American names. A difficult one was the name of neighbor Kris's father, "Vern," which he heard as "Barn." After changing it to "Burn with a V for Victory," he remembers it now as "Victory Fire." Let's hope this doesn't turn into another Bluebird Sandwich situation.

Vern, for his part, can remember and pronounce Shingo's name, but usually refers to him as "The Dalai Lama."

When it comes to travelling the island, Shingo's better than both of us at remembering how to go. He's got directions down pat and a strong memory for landmarks. He can look at a map once and re-member it indefinitely, whereas I can't even read and absorb it to begin with. I can and do ask directions, though, but like most men, he'd rather die.

There's a long "You'd better not forget!" list that shakes its finger at both of us regarding the all-important details of home maintenance which support our off-grid life:

Don't forget to put oil and water in the car.

Don't forget to check the solar system batteries and add water if they need it.

Switch propane tanks; buy propane.

Defrost the fridge; make room for some actual food in the freezer.

Change the outdoor water filters.

Put gas and carburetor cleaner in the generator; change its oil.

Add beneficial microbes to the cess pool: tell them to "*Mange la merde!*" (Pardon my French.)

Get a safety check on the car before August.

Have the chimneys cleaned.

Order wood.

Clean the generator air filter and spark arrester.

Replace the kitchen sink drinking-water filter when the little green light goes red.

And – please, oh, please – don't forget to empty the rat trap.

It's no problem remembering to take our non-compostable garbage to the local dump. A tell-tale aroma reminds us if we don't. But now, with reduced days of operation due to county budget shortfalls, we have to remember which days the dump is open – Tuesday, Friday, and Sunday – and get there before the aroma becomes too tell-tale.

To most of our friends who live in cities this all sounds burdensome, but after five years of rubber-boot life we've fallen into the rhythm of the dance, and the bandleader is a calendar on which everything is dat-ed and slated.

Once in a while we get sloppy and act as though we're living on the grid. But having the lights go out in the middle of dinner, or the fridge defrost unexpectedly, gets us back on our toes.

Then there's the twice yearly run-through by Michael McMillan of Michael's Repair, the man who knows everything about solar-electric and water systems, propane fridges and stoves, and how to keep them healthy. He does an inspection of our off-grid equipment every six months. If something has slipped our minds, he'll catch it. If it never entered our minds, he'll catch it.

On one visit he checked the solar panels for algae, found a fine film on the older ones, and scrubbed them clean, thereby increasing our solar energy by as much as 5%. Last time he discovered four dead batteries and replaced them, bringing the solar system back to normal, allowing us to stop scratching our heads in front of the voltmeter.

This man, who gets up on the roof, and feels just as comfortable under the house, and can and does fix anything and everything, is the same man who puts on a tuxedo and sings classical music in a Big Island choral group which travels the world. He's even played Carnegie Hall.

Are you impressed? I am.

Speaking of world tours: do you know who Justin Bieber is? If you're a pre-teen, you know perfectly well that he's a sixteen year old Canadian singer-songwriter and you're swooning at the very mention of his name. If you live on the Big Island, you'd spend lots of your parents money to fly to one of his Honolulu concerts. When you grow up, it'll be his music which reminds you of your first kiss, or who you danced with at the Junior Prom, not *Earth Angel,* not *Stayin' Alive,* not *Billie Jean,* not *Who Let The Dogs Out.* You'll never forget him.

Not being a tween myself, and never having heard of Justin Bieber, I nodded and smiled politely when our soon-to-be-thirteen-year-old friend Catharine Gussman's voice went up a few notches when saying his name.

I looked him up online so as not to be out-of-the-loop, but Justin Beiber's not my idea of a heart-throb. Though totally talented, he's too little and too cute.

For fall-in-love-fabulous talk to me about Elvis Presley, who was more tongue-tyingly handsome in real life than he was on screen; or Steve McQueen, especially in strong and silent mode; or Jean Paul Belmondo, what was it about his mouth? And you can always talk to me about Jet Li, former kung fu champion of China, whose martial arts moves are better than ballet, especially in his films from the 1990's.

None of these names will send Catharine's voice any higher. And it's not a question of "how soon they forget." She's not that well acquainted with my idols in the first place.

Even her mother, Yoko, is not familiar with most of the actors and actresses I worked with on *The Love Boat*. She'd been asking me about those days and I started dropping names – Esther Williams, Fernando Lamas, Sid Caesar, Nanette Fabray, Helen Hayes, Pearl Bailey, Lorne Greene – but she didn't know any of them. I thought everyone knew who Mae West was, but not. Likewise Ray Bolger. It needed to be explained that he's the scarecrow in *The Wizard Of Oz*.

Yoko can be excused from any *Love Boat* familiarity test since she grew up in Japan, but not knowing the stars in question made stories about them less fun to tell.

Like the time Ray Bolger told me some of his best scenes were cut from *The Wizard Of Oz* and that it would have been a much better movie if they'd been left in.

And that Mae West was so ancient and deaf when she played *The Love Boat* that she had a dialogue coach, who read her lines to her, wired to her hearing device – but she'd then deliver the line in her own, inimitable, forever-sexy way.

And that every star's ego was easily bruised: you had to watch your words . . .

Cyd Charisse, for example, was playing a French woman who'd been separated during the second world war from the love of her life, an American, played by Craig Stevens. Both show up on a cruise but he's reluctant to speak to her because she's travelling with a younger French man whom he supposes to be her lover. As it turns out, (you guessed this, didn't you?) the younger man is their son. (Are you crying? You're supposed to be.)

I thought the casting for this segment was exceptional. The actor playing the young Frenchman looked so much like the "parents" he really could have been their offspring.

I said this to Cyd Charisse who bit my head off: "Don't be ridiculous!" she snapped, "I'm too young to have a son that age!"

One of the names Yoko did recognize was that of Jaclyn Smith of *Charlie's Angels*, who may have received a tennis court for appearing on *The Love Boat*. Her husband had discreetly put the word out that that's what it would take. Since every actor on the show was supposedly paid the same amount, "scale," ABC had a slush fund which bought expensive treats for guests who could raise the ratings just by showing up. I don't know if she got her tennis court, but she did show up. And she did raise the ratings.

In some cases, special guests were allowed to take home props or wardrobe. Film actress Eleanor Parker, famous before my time, whose years of mouthful-of-marbles voice training caused her to pronounce her own name "Eleanoah Pahkah," kept the fake giraffe coat she wore on a special wedding cruise to Alaska.

She played the mother of the bride whose father, an alcoholic social drop-out, enacted by Ray Milland, boards the ship in San Francisco, wanting to wish his daughter well.

On deck, wearing her giraffe coat, she spots him and says her line, "What the Hell is he doing here?" which, with her highly dramatic delivery, came out "Wha th' HELL is HE doing HEAAHHH!!!"

I've always wished for a chance to say that, and to say it like she did, but, so far it hasn't been in the script.

Originally, the executive producers of *The Love Boat* planned to use only television stars on the show, but soon discovered that they were too busy shooting their own hit series. So we started using older movie stars like Ginger Rogers, and June Allyson, Arlene Dahl and Alice Faye, and second-banana comedy actors like Louis Nye and Don Knotts, and singers Sonny Bono, Frankie Avalon, and Robert Goulet, to the delight of our audience and ourselves: these were performers we all loved. Effervescent favorites like Charo and Ethel Merman returned season after season in semi-regular roles. It was gratifying to think that we re-started the careers of quite a few performers who hadn't been heard from in a while.

By its consistent high ratings and loyal following, *The Love Boat* flipped the old Hollywood adage "How soon they forget" on its ear. It proved that audiences don't forget the people who've entertained them. It made skeptical network executives re-examine their desires for "new, newer, newest" and admit that "old, older, oldest" can add up to landslide ratings as it did on *The Love Boat*. The program itself just keeps on going, being seen somewhere in the world, in some language, always.

So many old TV shows, movies, music, films, and books have new lives because of the internet, iPhones, iPods, iPads, satellite radio, CDs, DVDs, Kindles, and the incredible number of cable and free television channels which must be filled from dawn to dawn with something to watch. On-demand streaming over the internet is becoming another picture window for everything that's ever been produced.

As America's and the world's population ages, perhaps it won't be just retro and antique entertainment and artifacts which come in for new appreciation, but retro and antique people.

Even if some of them tap their heads and say, "My memory's so bad. I used to know that song Edith Piaf was famous for, but . . ."

If this happens to you, just excuse yourself and go to your computer of choice. After a few moments you can return triumphantly to the conversation.

"Got it! *La Vie En Rose!*"

Now that we have Google, who needs a good memory, anyway?

HOW OLD IS OLD?

Our DVD Player was only four years old when Elen, the library technician at the Mountain View Public & School Library, suggested we replace it with a new one, which we did.

It wasn't so much a question of age as it was a matter of "new and improved," she said. The newer DVD players featured better laser technology which would give us a normal viewing experience, whereas the "old" weak-lasered one caused movies to flip and flap, usually at a moment of high excitment:

He's finally going to kiss her! – flap, flap, flap. She's falling off the cliff! – flip, flip. "Frankly, my dear, I don't give a" – flap.

I grew up in the age of built-in obsolescence. But today, there's no need to build obsolescence in. Things go obsolete before their manufacturers even want them to.

Ongoing waves of new and improved send formerly fabulous technology to the dump . . . okay, the recycling center.

My Technics state-of-the-art record player, a thing of beauty in brushed aluminum, could be wall-mounted in a section of shelving to play records at 33 or 45 rpm. You could watch the records being played, vertically, through its clear acrylic cover. How up-to-the-minute!

It was connected to a compact Aiwa stacked sound system, with a tiny tape deck, radio, tuner, and amp, which, with the help of a couple of Bose speakers, provided the ultimate in genuine stereo sound.

But most of us don't have records any more, and, here in the rainforest, we don't use tape because it goes moldy, so all of the above became so passe I couldn't even give it away. It's been replaced by an all-in-one radio/CD player – a "boom box," if you please – and CDs.

Likewise, our outdated cube of a television set and its matching VCR tape deck has been made redundant by a Samsung flat-screen LCD unit with Tri-Surround sound, and the newly unflappable DVD player. A bonus for us off-grid types from this new technology is that it uses less electricity than its forbears.

But wait! What's this about high definition TV, Blu-ray disc reader/writers, and 3D TV? It sounds as though our new viewing equipment is already technologically "old."

And our phones? Come on! It took two wrong moves to finally find the phone system, T-Mobile, which works well in the mountains. It gives good reception even in a storm and I can use my handset as a modem for the internet.

The internet connection is pokey. Somewhere between dial-up and DSL, it doesn't allow me to watch videos because they take too long to load: the sending party will drop the connection. But I don't mind. There are only so many hours in a day, and I don't want to take the time to watch videos on my computer. I'm using it to write.

Shingo is yearning for an iPhone, which our neighbors own and love. You can watch videos on it. You can buy and listen to music. You can play games; access the internet; use it as a musical instrument; use it as a camera; send photos back and forth in real time; e-mail with it; text and Twitter. It doesn't take a crystal ball to see a smart-phone in his future.

Meanwhile, Luddite that I am, I still haven't found out how to get or send a text message, or take a picture with my own phone, though I've had it for years.

I don't know how to pick up "call waiting" either.

I deny that this is because of my age. It just seems unnecessary. I have voice mail: leave me a message.

Am I being a curmudgeon like my Uncle Mac at 80? When answering machines first came on the scene, he adamantly refused to leave messages: "I'm not talking to a machine!" he'd say, and hang up.

The switch to a new phone may be inevitable for both of us, but what am I supposed to do with all these "old" phones we've accumulated since we moved here?

The calling-card phones we bought to manage our move weren't transferrable to a more permanent plan at Verizon. We had to buy new ones which never did get decent reception. Yes, that was me out on Road Nine, hoisting an umbrella against the rain, while trying to make a phone call to my bank.

Then the new ones couldn't be used at our next phone company, T-Mobile: we had to get newer new ones.

Those four Verizon phones are illegal now because they don't have GPS – global positioning satellite capability, which the police use to find you when you dial 911 – so they can't even be donated.

If we were prone to violence, we could probably get a charge out of bouncing these used-to-be-the-latest communication devices off a rock. But that's not going to happen. They'll probably just sit, indefinitely, with their owners' manuals, in my closet, where they've been since they became unusable.

Like my Sony land phone which, I have to admit, is pretty old. I've had it since the 1980's. There's no land line here, so we can't use it, but I'm not getting rid of it.

It's so well designed. Its sleek modern face features large numbers and letters on big round buttons. It has a little red light that blinks when you have messages. Its receiver is lightweight and comfortable to use (does it sounds strange to you that a phone once came in two pieces?).

You can't take a picture with it. It didn't replace our Nikon camera, or the Canon Sureshot, enhanced by Photoshop, which did. You can't play a game on it, or use it to type a note to someone, but I don't see that as a drawback. It's a phone which sticks to its core business of phoning. I like that in a phone. I'm going to keep it as long as I live. And if I ever have a land line again, I'll hook it up and be glad I did

My sewing machine, no getting away from it, is old: older than old. It was a gift from that Los Angeles landlady, the one with the Spring-o-later mules, in 1967. And it was already a part of history. It once was a treadle machine, like one my grandmother used at her off-grid summer cottage in Northern Quebec, later converted to electricity. Its motor was patented in 1922, so I'm guessing the sewing arm may be older still.

I asked Shingo for a new sewing machine for my last birthday and he bought me a brand new Singer. It's still in the box. I've tried to make the switch, but it makes me feel so guilty I just can't do it.

First, I must find a good home for the veteran White machine I've been using for forty-three years, but, to tell the truth, I haven't been trying.

I have an unreasonable attachment to this battle-scarred war-horse, which only sews forward, not backwards, will not make a buttonhole, and has an electric cord that's so worn out it will give you a shock if you don't wear rubber-soled shoes to push the foot pedal. It will, however, sew through four thicknesses of leather, and has made more clothes and curtains and tablecloths and upholstered more furniture than it ever expected to.

I've often thought of converting it back to a treadle. Using your feet to power the machine, as we did at Nana's cottage, was a rhythmic, pleasant way to sew. It would also give me bragging rights for saving extra electricity off the grid. Two people I know have treadle tables mouldering on their properties here in East Hawaii. Should I ask for one of them?

I'd like to tell you about my Merrow Overlock, too, another sewing machine I've had forever, but I'm afraid you'll be bored. Enough with the sewing machines, right? Just let me say that if you look at the inside of your tee-shirt, this is the machine that binds two pieces of double-knit together and cuts off the excess. Mine was manufactured between 1926 and 1927! When I checked the internet for The Merrow

Machine Company, found their website, and e-mailed them to discover its age, they replied: "Your machine is as old as dirt."

No wonder they've been in business since 1838. What a sense of humor. And they keep up with the times. They have a happening website. You can find them on Facebook. Most importantly, they make things that last.

Sewing machines and marriages: sometimes they do, sometimes they don't, but it's so satisfying if they do. You already know how they work. You don't need to keep referring to the instructions. And if, on top of it, they keep you in stitches, how bad can that be?

If you're good at subtraction, you know I'd already hit the half-century mark when Shingo and I met. He was forty-six. He claims I robbed the cradle.

For just two months and one week of every year, I'm five years older than he is and he loves to remind me of it. As soon as his birthday rolls around, I'm only four years older and I love to remind him of it.

I'm the only female who's lived with him for more than twenty years, including his mother, step-mother, first wife, and daughter. And he's the only one who's put up with me for more than two decades.

Having met in middle age, we were perhaps more patient than we were as younger people, not as ready to storm out the door.

Still, we've never treated marriage as a noose. We let each other have plenty of space: to travel alone, to nap when sleepy, to be in a frenzy when you just have to finish a project ignoring all else.

Now, as seniors, we both work harder at our cross-cultural love affair because this is the final chapter and we know it.

It's more urgent now to say, "Thank you," "You're wonderful," "I'm sorry," or "I love you." It's more fun than ever to make each other laugh.

But let's get back to the issue of concern. Let's resolve the question: How old is OLD?

I asked Google about old age and got unexpectedly entertaining results.

"The age at which a person is old is always a bit older than *you* are," says Jeffrey Love, of AARP, in a 2009 *New York Times* article.

The same article quotes a survey by the Pew Research Center in which younger people said old begins at 68. But few over 65 agreed. They said old begins at 75.

Going further: in *Growing Old In America*, a report based on that Pew study, adults under 30 said old starts at 60. Adults between the ages of 30 and 49 said old begins at 69.

The Ohio State University Department of Aging says some gerontologists make a distinction between the "young-old" (ages 55 to 74) and the "old-old" (ages 75 and older). Still others add a "middle-old" category.

And here's a definition direct from Planet Woo Woo: Professor Timothy Salthouse of the University of Virginia was quoted on the internet in March of 2009 by BBC Health as saying that old age begins when top brain performance begins to decline. According to him, old begins at 27!

The Pew study showed that only one thing is certain when it comes to admitting to being elderly: most people insist that none of the research that's been done applies to them.

Me, too. At 70 I don't feel much different than I did at 50 or even younger. I certainly don't feel old. Even young-old doesn't sound like a good description of me, to me.

What's "old" mean, anyway? I'll take Webster's usages "mature in judgement," "wise," "having long experience or practice"; but flatly reject "not new," "worn out by age," "belonging to the remote past." Hey! My past isn't *that* remote.

Shingo, on the other hand, was convinced he was old when sciatica levelled him. He was sure he'd never come back to his former self, able to lift and carry and climb and work long hours without feeling it.

I told him he was full of baloney. He's always complained of being exhausted after a day of hard work. "Almost dead!" has been his oft-repeated motto as he flops down on the sofa.

His memory of younger days is illusory, picturing a non-existent time in which he's always vigorous and unflagging.

But by now, he's returned to his former physical strength almost completely. Exercise and herbs are keeping sciatica in check. In the last two weeks he's picked up and carried rocks from a roadside site to the trunk of our car and from there to a new pond he's making in the back yard. He's doing it little by little, sometimes with help from the neighbors, but he's doing it.

Yesterday, he installed mesh covers on the gutter that empties into the pond, so leaves won't wash into it. This called for a tall wobbly ladder and a heart-thumping balancing act. I know people half his age who wouldn't have tackled it.

In all the writing I've run into lately about old age, I haven't seen much mention of "over ninety." I suspect it's because most writers and most people in segmented American society don't know anyone that old.

That's a real shame. The over-nineties we're fortunate to know here on The Big Island are beyond inspirational.

If you want to feel like a lazy slob, go hang out with Mrs. Watanabe, 94, at the Obon Carnival at Taishoji Temple. You can find her serving shave-ice and hot dogs in the food booth, where she never sits down.

Meet Mrs. Tanimoto, 92, once a month, in Taishoji's kitchen, where she'll be helping to prepare traditional foods to feed the congregation following services. She's easy to recognize: she looks like a white-haired teenager and giggles just as readily. You won't see her sitting down either.

We recently bought six different jams and jellies, which she home-made from home-grown fruit, and donated to raise money for the temple. Do you know how many hours of work six different jams and jellies represents?

After a long day in the kitchen, her daughter tells us, she complained that her legs felt tired.

"Mom," her daughter said, "You have to remember, you're not seventy any more."

And then there's Mrs. Saito, 93, singing impossibly rangy Japanese language Buddhist hymns as a member of Taishoji's choir, then later, teaching younger women to make an intricate lei from the buds of white ginger.

Mrs. Saito was the first woman president of the temple, a ground-breaking appointment.

Mrs. Tanimoto, who's also in the choir, and also tirelessly works the Obon food booth, has run just about everything at Taishoji, including Sunday School, with style and selflessness.

These brave women survived and surmounted the strictures of their day: "a women's place is in the home"; the caste system for immigrant workers and their families during sugar plantation days; the traumas of World War II when their parents, local leaders of Japanese ancestry, even those born in the United States, were snatched from their homes and interned as enemy aliens in camps in the islands and on the mainland; and the devastating loss of life when the segregated 100th/442nd Infantry, made up overwhelmingly of Japanese-Americans, who volunteered to fight in WWII to redeem the reputations of their friends and families, became the most decorated regiment for its size in the history of the United States armed forces – meaning most of them did not come home.

Mrs. Saito witnessed the bombing of Pearl Harbor while sitting on a hill in Oahu, where she lived at the time. She says, "I just prayed that it wasn't the Japanese. But it was."

These over-ninety girls have lived out and out-lived the Industrial Revolution, as cars, trucks, railroads, airplanes, telephones, electric lights, electric stoves, refrigerators, radios, movies, phonographs, photographs, electric tools, television, washing machines, clothes dryers, dishwashers, vacuum cleaners, electric irons, pop-up toasters, garbage disposals, (long list isn't it?), rice cookers, microwave ovens, plug-in coffee pots, electric and electronic sewing machines, (thank Mr. Edison and his 1,093 patents for much of it), solar cells, satellites, modems, word processors, cell phones, digital cameras, cordless tools, personal computers, and (gasp!) the internet, became commonplace.

Being over ninety, they're among the first human beings to be "on the grid."

They grew up in a world without supermarkets, Starbucks, and not even one MacDonald's. Nobody had been to the moon. There was no such thing as "the pill."

They lived through Prohibition, the 1929 stock market crash, the Great Depression, atomic bombs dropped on Hiroshima and Nagasaki, two devastating tsunamis in Hilo, bursting Big Island volcanos which wiped out entire neighborhoods, the Kennedy and King assassinations, the tragedy of 9/11, and on and on.

In challenging times they married, had children, and overcame wartime hardship by raising food, learning to drive, and going out to work.

After the war they continued to be "career girls," working mothers, but still found time to form community organizations and contribute to them by volunteering their talents.

They were founders of their Buddhist temple and worked hard to help it grow.

They honored their parents and took care of them as they aged.

They were good neighbors and friends. They still are. And they're still volunteering.

Even though they're over 90, I couldn't call them "old." Made to last, you bet. Vital, yes. Busy, yes. If you want to invite them to lunch or dinner, better book ahead.

Knowing them, and all the other go-get-'em over-sixties, over-seventies, and over-eighties we meet in Hilo, I have to say that "old" is just a label.

And it's the label itself that is . . . (here, let's agree with Webster's definition: "not new," "worn out by age," "belonging to the remote past") . . . "old."

MADE TO LAST

Native Hawaiian hapuu fern trees have been around since paleolithic times. Since they form the tall and hairy, frilly, ferny setting of our jungle garden, we get to observe their personality traits, traits which, no doubt, have increased their longevity.

First of all, they're interesting. They've kept their pre-historic look. Their air of "I used to pal around with dinosaurs" fires the imagination, causing humans to feel protective, as they are these days toward the hapuu. Good thing, because hapuu bark is the perfect medium for potting orchids and if somebody wasn't watching out for them they'd be carved up and shipped all over the world as they once were.

They're resilient: if one falls over, and they do, it will raise its fronds up from the ground and start growing vertically from there, looking for all the world like an enormous snail holding a bright green umbrella.

Place a stone-dead, moss-covered hapuu stump in the landscape on which to plant an orchid and it will soon surprise you with its own new lacy-green growth.

These tree ferns have always been useful to humans. Their silky branch-hairs provided pillow stuffing and wound dressing and embalming material to Hawaiians of old. You can even eat their unfurled fronds.

I learned from Rodney Nishino and Elaine Miura at Taishoji Temple to make "kakuma," cooking hapuu fronds plantation style, boiling and peeling them outdoors to avoid their eye-stinging acidic steam, soaking and rinsing for at least five days in cool water, slicing and chopping them into small thin rectangles, then adding ginger, and onions, and sugar, and seaweed, and soy sauce, and sweet sake, plus a shot of vinegar, to make a delicious, even educational, potluck dish.

Back in the day, the Taishoji community used to gather at the Miura family's home to make it, then sell it at Buddhist gatherings on other islands to earn money for the temple. These days the airlines charge too much to carry the product inter-island, so a cherished custom has come to an end.

Historically, kakuma was called "the food of death," but not because it was a famine food or because it would poison you. It just took too many days to make.

This food-of-death name was a typical Hawaiian joke, just good fun, based on the idea that if you were really hungry you could croak before dinner was ready.

For faster food, there's chicken.

The Red Junglefowl coming and going in our back yard, have been feeding humans, here, for more than a thousand years.

The sailing canoes they rode to Hawaii arrived between 400 and 1000 CE. That would be between 600 and 1,200 years before the Mayflower made it to Plymouth Rock.

That's a lot of menus to be on. But they haven't disappeared. They're obviously made to last.

We eat a lot of chicken. But no Moa, no Red Jungle Fowl.

Currently a whole chicken at the market costs from $10 to $15. But don't even hint about bringing Yolanda to the table.

"She's getting nice and plump."

"How do you pluck a chicken?"

Comments like these have Shingo with his fingers in his ears.

He'd never get a good night's sleep if he had to kill a chicken from our back yard. He wants to take care of them, not eat them.

Anyway, I've been wondering: Might characteristics which appear to have lengthened life in nature be qualities which we humans, hoping for extra years, could copy?

Even with just two teachers it may be possible to get some helpful ideas.

From Hapuu Sensei . . .

"Be interesting. Tell your dinosaur stories and your food of death joke."

"Be resilient. If you fall over, get up. Start again from where you are."

"Be surprising. Grow a new frond, get a new outfit. When they've counted you out and are planning to use you as a planter, come back wearing bright green."

"Be useful. Make jam. Better yet, make kakuma."

And from Moa Sensei . . .

"Go to Shingo's back yard. He'll never kill you."

Though this advice may not look like a foolproof roadmap for our own endurance, if followed it would surely make our years as elders less predictable. It might help us in old age (whatever that is) to be the icing on the cake instead of the crumbs on the plate, someone to spend good times with: being part of a community, respected, even loved, is a scientifically recognized life extender.

As models of durability, researchers point to the inhabitants of The Republic of Abkhazia, formerly a region of Soviet Georgia. Into their eighties and nineties, they're still working in their gardens, riding horseback, and bathing in icy streams. In a *Time Magazine* article, anthropologist Dr. Alexander Leaf attributes their vigor to a high protein diet, exercise, and the right DNA.

But Soviet researchers tell of an elderly man who had never been sick who was forced to move from his Abkhazian village. He quickly began to wither until brought back to family and friends.

Do we need scientists to tell us this? Haven't we all had relatives removed from their usual haunts because they weren't coping on their own, whose lights have dimmed, then gone out?

If you want my opinion, it's not just about leaving home. And it's not about the quality of care they get. I think they slip away because life's no fun any more, because nobody's laughing and nobody's clapping.

Granted, not everyone will win the Nobel Prize in their eighth decade like Doris Lessing and 11 other laureates; or an Oscar, like Myrna Loy or Groucho Marx.

And not everyone will be roaring into space aboard a shuttle as Senator and astronaut John Glenn did in 1998 at age 77.

Hardly anyone will be hosting *Saturday Night Live* as Betty White did at 88.

But applause, fun, and laughter are important to folks in their final innings. They, as much as any of us, require it. It makes having lived and suffered through a long life that much more acceptable.

I saw a wheelchair-bound man of great age, who could no longer speak, in the patio at Lifecare Center in Hilo, surrounded by a daughter and several of his grandchildren, one of whom held up his brand-new great-grandchild for him to see, a recognition that without him none of them would have existed.

His lighthearted grandkids, ranging from late teens to new mother, were joking amongst themselves, and though he couldn't join in their laughter, he was bathed in the sound of their happiness, which always included him. I sensed that he knew it.

Aside from good health, I think laughter is a main ingredient in any recipe for longevity, more life-sustaining, even, than Jacques Cousteau's scuba gear, or Elizabeth Taylor's jewels.

That's why I'm lucky to have Shingo as a partner. He constantly makes me laugh.

He's physically funny . . .

He'd been trying to change the place where he feeds Yolanda but she didn't understand. So, the other morning, I saw him, this tall, thin, shaved shiny-bald, gently aging Zen priest, bobbing over the new spot, doing a perfect job of imitating a chicken pecking.

Despite my explosion of laughter, Yolanda caught on right away and began to eat.

Shingo, grinning proudly from ear to ear, flashed me a V for victory sign

If we're talking about sumo wrestling, suddenly he'll be the new grand-champion yokozuna, slapping his (non-existent) huge belly and throwing salt as he gets into the ring, crouching and posturing before his bout with yours truly, a smaller, less menacing, but nevertheless, fierce opponent.

Give him an umbrella and some koto music and he becomes a coyly alluring geisha dancer.

But only at home. He doesn't realize his talents and will rarely perform in public.

He's verbally hilarious . . .

Once, in L. A., we were stuck in nighttime traffic, moving at a crawl toward a mid-city destination. Neon signs, glowing all around us, advertized goods and services for sale, overlapping and nullifying each other to the point where natives no longer notice. But Shingo was paying attention:

"Why LIQUOR?" he asked, meaning "What's the etymology of the word?" Before I could answer, he asked "Why DONUT? Why TAXI?"

Without a dictionary, I had no answers, but he did.

"MOTEL," he said, as we inched forward towards another sign, "I know that one. Meaning is MOTOR/HOTEL."

"Yes," I said, "But why MOTOR?" (hoping to turn the tables on the English quiz) "Why HOTEL?"

"MOTOR is CAR," he said with assurance, "HOTEL is HOT and TELL. Drive to there, get warm, please say to friends."

Near our last L. A. loft there was a billboard on the street which advertised "The Score, A Gentlemen's Club."

This was a strip joint, lap-dance kind of place, with pretentions of class. Next to a much-larger-than-life photo of a semi-nude female with a come-hither look were the words "Complimentary Lunch."

Shingo took this to mean that while you were having lunch a beautiful girl would pay you compliments, such as, "You look very nice today."

I hope he's made to last.

There's every possibility. His father lived to 95 and his mother to 88. He's got the genes. We'll just have to wait and see what he makes of them.

Bob Newhart, my old boss, is made to last. He's in his eighties now, so you might say he's already lasted. He's still doing stand-up comedy according to his Facebook page. He's on Twitter, too, so you can follow him. He made his latest film in 2008 at the age of 79. A new generation gets to meet this comedians' comedian.

Bob Hope, another comedy genius, lived to be 100, and took his last USO show on the road at 87.

George Burns made 100, too, and kept working until he was 99. He wrote 10 books in his later years and at 89 filmed a television series for CBS: *George Burns Comedy Week*. The ingrates cancelled him after one season, but that's show business.

Why did these venerable comedians keep at it? Were they having fun? Surely they didn't go to all the trouble, the gathering of material from writers, the production planning, the rehearsals, the last minute changes, the re-learning of scripts, the endless challenges of entertaining, just for ego gratification or for money. They already had plenty of both.

Assuming they *were* having fun, did it lengthen their lives?

Dr. Robert Butler should know. One of the world's leading authorities on growing old; founder of the gerontology department at Mt. Sinai Medical Center in New York; founder and first director of the National Institute on Ageing; Pulitzer Prize-winning author; and writer, at age 83, of *The Longevity Prescription*, he was interviewed by Joshua Tapper of *The New York Times* in August of 2010 and surprised the reporter by asking him how long *he* wanted to live.

"As long as I enjoy life," said Mr. Tapper, suddenly worrying that his answer was too glib.

But Dr. Butler replied, "I think you've said it right. You want to live as long as you enjoy life."

He added: "That's the real truth."

I have one more story to tell you about a person who was made to last. His name was Burt Mustin.

If you ever watched 50s, 60s, or 70s TV, in original airings, re-runs, or on *Nick At Nite,* you'd know him, maybe not by name, but you'd know his face. He was one of the most familiar character actors in the United States.

Born in 1884, he had a long career as a car salesman in Pennsylvania. But he always wanted to be a professional actor and vowed that when he retired at 65 he'd pursue his dream. He trained in amateur theater in his spare time and when the moment came for him to go pro, he was ready. He moved to Hollywood at age 67 and never stopped working. In comedy, he became the new old face.

He appeared in 27 films including *Snow White and the Three Stooges, Cat Ballou,* and *Mame,* and a long list of television shows with regular roles on *Leave It To Beaver* – he was Gus, the fireman; *The Andy Griffith Show* – he was Jud Crowley; *All In The Family* – he was Harry Feeney; and *Phyllis,* on which he played the boyfriend-then-husband of Mother Dexter until shortly before his death at 92.

Even as a late, late, late bloomer, he made people laugh for 25 years and they're laughing still.

If he didn't enjoy life I'd like to know who did.

DEATH IN THE BOONIES

I'm a killer: a rat trapper, mosquito masher, slug slayer, fruit-fly eradicator. Under my hand many a creature has been terminated with extreme prejudice.

I take it as a duty to squish a neon-green leaf-hopper before it takes a nip out of an orchid bud. It won't eat the whole thing, just take one bite where bud joins stem, which makes the long-awaited flower-to-be drop off. That luminous little bug must join its ancestors.

I helped bump off thirteen goldfish. That wasn't intentional. Trying to be helpful, Shingo and I decided to change the water in their small pond, not realizing you can't change it all at once. If you do, the fish expire, not suddenly but slowly, of diseases they contract because their environment has changed too radically. Their scales fall off, their stomachs bulge, they lose their balance, and eventually you find them belly-up.

Eight of the thirteen deceased fish had grown from guppy-size to koi-like on our watch. We'd named the largest after famous sumo wrestlers from Hawaii, "Akebono," "Konishiki," "Musashimaru." As each one died, we became more and more distraught, buying every pond medication, trying to save them, but it was too late. Five of them were born at our place which doubled our guilt. We have a forest full of fish graves. They're unmarked, but we know they're there.

I'm a coqui frog eliminator, too, but I have no bad conscience about that. They need enemies on this island to keep their numbers in check. Unfortunately, my anti-coqui activities aren't doing much to control the population.

Considering that a little over five years ago we started with one tree frog and that now there are hundreds, maybe thousands, singing "co-QUI," "co-QUI," at 70 to 90 decibels throughout the forest, our attempts to get rid of them can't be described as a win.

It's like having a full orchestra of nothing but piccolo players, hitting the same two notes, at random, outside your window all night, into the morning. Sometimes they rehearse in the afternoon.

What we need is coqui birth control, or a coqui preacher who teaches abstinence. It's their mating call, after all, and the success of it, which is destroying Big Island quiet. But, so far, neither coqui condoms nor coqui fundamentalism has arrived.

Until then, there's murder. And it comes in various forms.

At first, back in 2007, we had a neighborhood effort to hand catch the tiny tree frogs, which are about the size of your thumbnail.

A group of six or seven or us, organized by forest ranger Rita Pragana, would go out at dusk on a given day and inspect our immediate area, listening along our roads for frog chirps.

A chirping frog is a male singing to attract a female who's buried in the ground. If she likes the sound of him, she'll join him in his tree and they'll do that thing.

First, we'd mark the suspected frog boudoirs with brightly colored tape, identifying assignation sites to return to, if necessary. We'd then close in, trying to find the serenading frog.

This was never easy because coquis are ventriloquists: they throw their voices. As soon as you think you've found one, and go there, the sound seems to come from somewhere else.

If you get too close, the frog stops chirping. And the night gets darker. And the frogs go higher up the trees (the better to broadcast to you, my dear), so you can't reach them even if you find them.

Nevertheless, using flashlights and the keen ears of Kristin and Shingo, two how-do-they-do-it? coqui finders, we'd catch four or five frogs a night, which we triumphantly put into Ziplock bags and the bag into someone's freezer, handing them a supposedly compassionate but unexpectedly Arctic end.

But, that's only four or five frosted frogs a week, not enough to make a difference.

We wanted to rain death on the coquis before they got a foothold in our neighborhood. Our frog czar, Rita, borrowed a machine from The County of Hawaii which would emulsify hydrated lime and keep it suspended in water. It had a long hose so we could traipse through empty fields and spray the woods beyond.

We, again, did this as a neighborhood, in the daytime, but the machine was so cumbersome and so hard to clean and such a nuisance to borrow and return that we only used it once. And the frogs kept multiplying.

Next came neighbor Taylor De Court's more mobile method. He modified a leaf blower and used it to spray dry lime powder into the woods.

Hearing success stories made Shingo want to try. He went completely hazmat, covered from head to foot in protective clothing, wearing goggles and a mask, to spray the lime around our house.

At one touch of the blower's on-switch, lime came poofing out in a giant cloud and infiltrated everywhere instantly. Though he was down at the back of the garden, I had to race to close the windows in the house because lime immediately drifted in. You could smell it, you could taste it: it ought to be hard on a coqui frog.

Under his plastic outfit, Shingo was sweating and lime was mixing with his perspiration, stinging him, so he had to keep taking everything off, washing his face and hands with cool water, then suiting up again and going back out. It took him several hours to complete his disagreeable chore and finally get cleaned up.

Then we waited for nightfall.

Dusk: no "co-QUI."

Dark: no "co-QUI."

Moonrise: no "co-QUI."

Bedtime: "Congratulations! No more coquis!

Wait a minute . . . what was that?"

"Co-QUI!!!"

Neighbor Ski has made over two hundred coqui traps out of PVC pipe and strapped them to the trees near his house. Males choose the pipe as a secure place (they wish) to mate with a female. She lays her eggs and then goes back into the ground. The male, a valiant-if-noisy house-husband, guards the eggs until they hatch.

So far Ski has trapped over 113 males, 11 females, and 32 clutches of eggs. He puts his full trap into a Ziploc, heads for the freezer, and turns the whole family into Icelanders.

But it hardly makes a dent. One female can lay 1,400 eggs a year.

Once, I found a clutch of about 30 to 40 coqui eggs and decided to eat them, reasoning that if they tasted like a fancy new island *hors d'oeuvre*, we'd all have a stronger motive for spending the time to find and collect them. But I couldn't bring myself to eat them raw. And boiled, they had no taste at all.

I offer this undeveloped idea, with no hope of personal gain, to anyone who's interested. If you're tough enough, or dumb enough, to take a raw bite, I respect you for your daring, pray for your wellbeing, and hope you make a million out of coqui caviar.

Our latest method of tree frog execution is a mixture of citric acid and water in a spray bottle. I've sprayed at least a dozen frogs in the last year, which dries the poor things out and turns them into coqui leather. But Shingo has to find them first. This requires co-ordination, but at the proper dusky hour, he's usually painting in his studio, I'm cooking, and no frog gets found even if it's co-QUIing its brains out.

It's not all failure, though. Last month we stumbled on a coqui orgy, going on under the tentlike top of our water catchment when a frog chirped at noon. (Perhaps it was having a complimentary lunch.)

In one hour, slowly lifting the edge of the top, we found and dispatched 8 frogs.

But our number one wish is that the wild chickens at our place will find coquis edible, absolving us of the need to rub them out.

That's correct, I said "chickens" plural.

We have three these days: Yolanda, and "A" and "B" – having had some highly emotional chicken moments in the past, we're afraid to name any more of them.

Worryingly, Betty has not returned to our place. Nor did four of her six chicks. Just the two, still small, came back after an absence of about a week. One looks like Yolanda's twin. The other is chocolate brown. That's B.

Instead of welcoming the newcomers, Yolanda saw them as rivals. She tried to chase them away from birdseed breakfasts, but then spent the rest of her day trying to be their buddy. (Can you say schizophrenic chicken?)

But as A and B grew bigger they learned to aggressively fend off Yolanda. Now, with a new balance of power, they're making friends, cuddling up together under the house when it's raining, loudly warning each other of whatever chickens loudly warn each other about.

None of these birds is pretty. Don't tell Shingo I said so, but they're a sorry looking lot. And none gives us an egg: they're too young. But we remind ourselves of their legendary-ness, of the famous long distance travels of their ancestors. We picture double-hulled canoes propelled by koa-wood paddles and sails woven from pandanus leaves, riding the turquoise ocean, carrying (ugly) chickens.

We're glad to see them every day, and fervently hope that Betty and the other four haven't become a mongoose's lunch. We assure each other they're just visiting someone else.

Meanwhile, we've noticed a slight lessening of coqui frogs.

People say that chickens will scratch them out of their leaf-litter daytime hiding places and dine on them. We think it may be happening. It's not like the frogs are gone or that there's the old velvety silence at night before they came. But it seems a bit better.

You'd need an untold number of chickens, though, to cause a coqui frog extinction, but that's what most Big Islanders, plagued by them, would probably wish.

It may seem odd to talk about extinction as a desirable thing in an era when people get so worked up about the subject, particularly in Hawaii which is known as the endangered species capital of the world.

There are 279 plants, 1 bat, 1 seal, 1 tree snail, 32 birds and 5 turtles on threatened or endangered lists, meaning that their numbers are now so small they could soon be defunct, demised, departed, as in "dodo."

That's on top of 28 birds, 72 snails, 74 insects, and 97 plants that have gone extinct in Hawaii in the last 200 years. And those are just the ones we know about.

We can convict Rikki Tikki Tavi and Mr. and Mrs. Rat for a great deal of bird and turtle reduction. So why doesn't somebody train these omnivorous pests to eat coqui frogs instead: dig them up in the day-time (Rikki), or climb up and eat them at night (Ratty)?

Mrs. Tavi has already taught herself and some of her children to turn stones over and eat the slug beneath at Pauline Weddle's home in Hilo. More than one generation has learned the trick. At Pauline's it's "So-long slugs." So why not "Toodle-oo coquis?" Anybody know an animal behaviorist?

In his book *A Short History of Nearly Everything,* author Bill Bryson, surprisingly, calls extinction an "important motor of pro-gress." He writes that, "on Earth, species death is, in the most literal sense, a way of life – 99.99 percent of all species that have ever lived are no longer with us."

The fiery Hawaiian Goddess, Pele, and her fellow gods and god-desses worldwide might agree that destruction, and sometimes total devastation, is necessary to avoid stagnation.

It creates a stage for change. As members of the British TV comedy series *Monty Python's Flying Circus* were often heard to say, "And now for something completely different . . ."

According to Bryson's research, Earth has seen five major and many smaller extinction episodes, each of which provided new condi-tions for dramatic leaps of life.

The last of the five big ones, the Cretaceous, caused when an aster-oid collided with Earth about 65 million years ago, finished off the dinosaurs and 70 percent of Earth's other creatures, but spared the lives of turtles, snakes, crocodiles and innumerable smaller animals, insects, and ocean dwellers. Some of these found niches in the new design of nature and prospered. For a time, he tells us, there were guinea pigs the size of rhinos and rhinos the size of a two story house.

We modern humans and our ape-like ancestors have apparently only been around for about 4 million years, but our predecessors still had to slip through the cracks of potential extinction from every imaginable large-scale catastrophy, from severe climate change during ice ages, twelve of them, and subsequent warming periods, to volcanic eruptions, earthquakes, tsunamis, destructive winds, famines, and plagues of various sorts, and we're not even talking about war.

Think of bubonic plague, "the black death," which killed 1/3 of Europe, 50 million people, in the Middle Ages, and didn't disappear completely until the 1600s when they figured out that fleas jumping off rats and onto humans were the carriers. Today we have AIDS and malaria still slaughtering much of Africa.

Shingo once knew a man from El Salvador who, to escape the civil war in his country, walked to the United States. It took him two years, stopping and working here and there, during which time he was illegal, exploited, and ducking the authorities, from Guatemala all the way up the west coast of Mexico.

Finally making it to Los Angeles, he got an ill-paid job making picture frames, rented an apartment, lived frugally, and bought a junk car.

On a beautiful sunny Southern California Sunday he drove through Beverly Hills, sightseeing the mansions of the stars on Sunset Boulevard, but was stopped by the police.

"Where did you come from?" asked the cop. "Where are you going?"

"That's a very philosophical question," said Shingo's friend.

Just to let you know, nothing bad happened. The policeman checked his driver's license and registration and let him go on his way. In time, he got his "green card," making him a legal resident of California. Still, he returned to El Salvador after the government offered amnesty to all the civil war participants they hadn't killed.

But the part of his story that's of interest to us here is the policeman's question: "Where did you come from? Where are you going?"

111

If 99.99 percent of all the life that was ever on Earth is extinct, where did it go? And where did all the new species that showed up later come from?

Author Bryson says it's all about atoms. In order for anything to be here "trillions of drifting atoms had to somehow assemble in an intricate and intriguingly obliging manner."

It's not as though our own atoms care about us or even know we're here, he says. They don't even know *they're* here. They're mindless particles, not even themselves alive. Yet somehow, he insists, for the period of our existence they will answer to a single overarching impulse, to keep us as us.

But when a human life, or any other life, is over, he says, "for reasons unknown, your atoms will shut you down, silently disassemble, and go off to be other things."

Author Bryson's elementary explanation agrees with the Buddhist understanding of inter-connectedness, of no separate self.

When Zen Master Thich Nhat Hanh looks at the page of a book, he points out that it not only took a tree to make it, but clouds, the water that came from the clouds, sunlight, earth and all the components it took to make a patch of dirt; the people who decided to cut down the tree and the millions of ancestors who birthed them into this world; the people who made the saw that cut down the tree and all *their* forebears; the people who own or are employed at the mill and all *their* ancestors: it's a story without a beginning and without an end.

The explosion of paper that comes from the tree carries an atomic message that's much more fascinating than any words that will ever be printed on it. That message is so big and so wonderous it's beyond description.

Each step of the way, the page of print was "something completely different," and, as the page ages and moulders and eventually disintegrates, it'll become something completely different again, and again, and again. Thinking of reincarnation in atomic terms, it takes on a whole new meaning.

And if you think of death and rebirth in terms of reassembling atoms, it means that nothing goes away, and nothing is ever wasted.

112

Those atoms, when they're finished being what they are, become something else. And when they're finished being that, they become something else. Have a look in your compost heap: it's mushrooms and maggots, and who-knows-what-used-to-be-what.

An internet website, Chem4Kids.com, provides a list of atoms' whereabouts: they're the building blocks of "elements, molecules, macromolecules, cell organelles, cells, tissues, organs, systems, organisms, populations, ecosystems, biospheres, planets, planetary systems with stars, galaxies, the universe." Whooo!

As mathematical cosmologist Dr. Brian Swimme, who specializes in evolutionary dynamics, suggests: If you leave a bunch of helium atoms alone for 13 billion years, you get zebras, and amoebas, and iron, and redwood trees . . . and everything else.

Considering all the work atoms have to do, we're lucky they decide to be us for a while.

But when they don't, when we finally flatline, an atom travel itinerary might include the transition from human body, to fire and ash, to ocean detritus, to fish food, to fish as human food, to nourished sperm plus nourished egg, to brand new human, with a sidetrip of smoke, gasses, and moisture, to air, clouds, and rain. And that's just within a generation, no thirteen billion years.

Another journey might make formerly human atoms into worm food, into a big juicy worm, into bird food, into bird droppings, into fertilized plants, into human food. That carrot might contain traces of your great-great-grandfather. That ant might be your aunt.

Something like this way of thinking informs the daily life of Buddhist monks in Tibet and elsewhere. They mean it when they say of a fellow monk, "He wouldn't hurt a fly." That's why.

Hawaiians, too, see everything and everyone as their relatives, so that all of life and every death commands an intimate respect.

They feel personal responsibility for the land, the ocean, plants, animals, the "aina." And when they take the life of something to sustain their own lives, they feel grateful in a way that we may never have experienced.

Though death comes to everyone and everything, in American society we generally don't like to talk about it.

My L. A. girlfriend's father, a former television producer-director, is, as she puts it, "way beyond his expiration date." She wants to help him put his affairs in order, yet finds it difficult to say the "D" word to his face.

The show business term "on tour," which describes an actor leaving town to take a show on the road, is a perfect substitute. She's using it when talking to him, to his wife, to insurance companies, and even medical people, to the point that they're all using it too. She says "When Dad goes on tour" is making an impossible conversation possible.

At our age, Shingo and I should have the conversation, too. There's paperwork which needs to be in place in case our atoms take a notion to try something new.

Lots of legalities surround the "D" word. This was brought home to us recently when a good friend passed away, and Queen's Medical Center in Honolulu, where he died, was not allowed to tell us so. They were legally prevented from giving any information about him to anyone who did not possess a signed Power Of Attorney (it's to protect his privacy).

This got us digging further, and we discovered that there are a number of documents which we ought to prepare, not just in case of d-d-d-death, but in case of that other "D" word – disability.

They are: A Durable Power of Attorney, which allows a trusted individual to make financial and medical decisions for you if you're incapable; a Health Care Proxy, which gives someone you trust the right to make decisions about your medical treatment and, guided by you, when to stop it; a Living Will, which details your financial and medical wishes; and an HIPAA Release, which allows a doctor to give information about your medical condition, or your on-tour-ness, to family members or others whom you designate (when our friend didn't live, we were eventually called by the person he'd named).

Married couples may not think they need these documents because they have a spouse or children to make decisions for them if something unexpected happens, but it's not that simple. To make an informed decision about the subject: Google *"Do You Have The Right Emergency Documents?"* by Laura Adams, October 25, 2010.

An equally important question, which Google can't answer, is "Do you know what you want to put in them?"

In Ireland, when someone dies, they say, "He got away from us." I asked Shingo, if he gets a nasty diagnosis, whether he wants to "get away" or not.

He took me in his arms and said, "Maybe I don't know." He means he doesn't know now, and maybe he won't know then. In acknowledging this with him, I had to have a good cry.

D-d-d-death has its own beauty: d-d-d-definitely. From the micro-death of a coqui frog in the freezer, to the mass extinction of species, to the individual death of a human being, there's something vast and mysterious going on. Before too long both Shingo and I will know more about it.

But meanwhile, I'm with Woody Allen who famously quipped, "I'm not afraid of death. I just don't want to be there when it happens."

TIDYING UP

I've heard that when you die your whole life flashes before your eyes.

Is it only the good parts?

If so, I'm sure to see that Hallowe'en party at Ben Samareh's loft in L. A. when Shingo and Vinh Luong and I dressed up as Buddhism's Three Poisons: Greed (full length gold sequins), Anger (red sequins), and Ignorance (black sequins), and went around offering glittery sprinkles of evil from vials we wore around our necks. Some people shied away from our enticements, saying, "Don't give me that stuff." But others said, "Yeah! Bring it on!"

Or is it only the bad parts?

I hope not. I'd hate to go out on a sour note. And the movie would be too one-sided.

Maybe I could fast-forward the bad parts. But probably not, huh?

By bad parts I don't mean things that happened, like my mother's death or 9/11/2001, over which I had no control. I'm talking about oats of mine that were a little too wild, times when I didn't do my best, moments I regret, memories that make me cringe.

Even though I'm hardly on my death bed, some of these moments have been cropping up lately, reminding me that this is the eleventh hour, that the time to tidy up my karma is now.

The Dalai Lama (the real one) says karma isn't kismet, it's not the same as fate. He says it's about cause and effect: every action we take or don't take has a direct effect on ourselves and someone or something else, and there's no getting off the hook by claiming that destiny had a hand in it. Likewise, borrowing from comedian Flip Wilson won't work with the Dalai Lama. Don't bother insisting "The Devil made me do it."

That we have karma in our own hands, that we're responsible for our actions and their outcomes, that we're always touching others, who are always touching us, and always touching each other, is such a hopeful message. It's a circular story. And the circle is infinite.

It means that even if we've made mistakes (and who hasn't?), even if we've blown something badly, we can clean up our act. We can atone in ways we never thought of before: wider ways.

His Holiness isn't the only one recommending it. Leaders of all religions suggest we think seriously about the effect of our time on Earth and how it's going to look when we exit, whether we're expecting to greet St. Peter, or planning to claim those 72 virgins.

My Zen teacher, Maezumi Roshi, described atonement as being "at one with" as opposed to "separate from."

No more "Me" and "You," "Us" and "Them," no more "Those Damn People" just "Us All."

Right away I had to say, "I'm not 'Us All' with Hitler."

"But you are," he said. "You're part of the vast ocean of dazzling light and so is he. *And* you're each an individual wave."

The more I thought about it, the more I discovered that my individual wave wasn't as different from Hitler's as I might have wished. I'd acted out the three poisons since birth. I took more than my share. I was full of rage. I killed. I lied to make myself look good. I loved power. I only shared to make points. It was obvious I had a long way to go in the atonement area.

Spreading the bald-faced lies told by *The Love Boat* – that you can fall in love on a five-day cruise and live happily ever after; that most American woman have bodies and ball gowns like movie stars; that you can solve just about any problem on your way back from Puerta

117

Vallarta – suddenly felt wrong. What were we selling to people in 93 countries and 29 languages?

I mentioned this to one of Maezumi's senior students, Joko Beck, Sensei, and her answer surprised me. "Nobody takes *The Love Boat* seriously," she said. "It's just fun. I enjoy it." I guess you could say she was "at one" with it.

Living in a semi-monastic setting at Zen Center of Los Angeles, you could look at your life in the mirror of meditation.

While seated silently, you learned, as a beginner, to count your breath. And if thoughts interfered, not to judge, but to return to the number "one." Just "one, two, three, four," count up to ten and start over, something your mother might have recommended when you were about to bop your brother for borrowing your little red tricycle without permission.

One of my questions about making amends, scrubbing the slate cleaner, was, "What if you harmed a person and now they're dead? How do you deal with that?"

The answer I got was, "Just start from here. Start from "one." Do better than you did, and if you can't pay back directly for the hurt you caused, find some other way to pay back."

This advice took an unreasonable number of years to make sense, but it finally sank in after 9/11 when a group of former alcoholics in a twelve-step program were featured on television. They'd all gone to New York City to clean up Ground Zero as part of their own amends to people they could no longer reach.

At Zen Center we'd cleaned up after the L. A. riots in 1992, when a jury acquitted the four policemen who'd beaten Rodney King so viciously.

The riots surrounded ZCLA with burning and looting, but somehow spared the center. Nearby shops and restaurants that we used to patronize, were trashed. My dentist lost everything when her three story building went up in smoke.

Mexican-American actor and social activist Edward James Olmos, one of the stars of *Miami Vice*, also famous for his role in the play about East L. A., *Zoot Suit,* said on the news, "I'll be at the park at

Olympic and Normandie at 7:00 tomorrow morning with my broom. Meet me there." And we did. The park was next door.

The cleanup was a perfect example of "Us All."

Zen Center's neighborhood was a cultural crossroads, with Koreans to the West, Hispanics to the East, African Americans to the South, and a mixture of whites and other Asians – Phillipinos, Thais, and Vietnamese – to the North. The immigrant Japanese, like the Jews they'd supplanted, were long gone from the neighborhood to different parts of the city. But everyone came to the cleanup, from East L. A. and Santa Monica, from Monterey Park and Beverly Hills. You had your shovel, someone who spoke only Spanish had the garbage bag, someone who spoke Korean had a wheelbarrow. It got done with smiles and handshakes. What a day!

But people had died in the riots. A Korean shop-owner in South Central was shot to death by rampaging locals. Later, it was revealed that he'd been sensitive to the community, kind and giving.

A white truck driver who happened to be at the wrong crossroads at the wrong time was beaten almost to death.

The perpetrators were caught, tried, and locked up in jail. That's supposed to be their punishment. But whether jail works as "atonement" or "amends" is another question.

At Zen Center we studied The Sixteen Bodhisattva Precepts. These are like the Ten Commandments with a few extra do's and don'ts. "Do Not Be Stingy," is a precept that might have been written especially for me. "Do Not Elevate Yourself and Put Down Others," is one I like. But, as in other religions, The Precepts begin with "Do Not Kill."

Lately, I'm back killing rats which love to sneak into our water-filter cabinet. They're easily attracted by dog-food bait, which gets them zapped in The Rat Zapper.

I once asked Joko Sensei about killing. Again, I was surprised by her answer. She didn't say, "Don't let killing even enter your mind." She said it was sometimes necessary, but that it was important to examine your motives and take responsibility for your actions. She'd had mice in her apartment and, at first, did nothing about it. But soon,

119

she was over-run. She needed to eliminate them and did. According to the Dalai Lama, even he smacks a mosquito now and then.

I've never killed a human, but plenty of humans have been killed in my name, and yours, and Maezumi Roshi's, and Joko Beck's, in wars intended to "increase our security and protect our way of life."

This Island of Hawaii is very military, a training ground for combatants currently headed to wars in Iraq and Afghanistan. It's a hard reminder to see their desert camouflage uniforms in tropical Hilo and know that they themselves could soon be killed.

Our ex-rats?

The Health Department applauds.

Some monks shudder.

I take responsibility for being comfortable that their atoms have gone off to re-assemble elsewhere.

I don't plan to put the rat trap away, either. I'll atone some other day, some other way.

Last week, the atoms in Shingo's computer re-assembled. He took the dead machine to a young man in Hilo who works with Macs, but nothing could be done. The hard-drive had suffered mechanical failure.

Shingo had the idea that something can always be salvaged from a seemingly deceased computer. But not in this case.

So he's grieving the loss of his data. And he's caught up in "if only."

"If only I'd kept a copy." "If only I'd had the machine serviced." "If only I'd bought a new one sooner, I could have transferred all that information."

This is 100% human, and 100% not Zen.

"If only" is as much of a trap as The Rat Zapper. It keeps us living in the past.

And yet we apply "if only" to relationships with parents, siblings, mates, children, lovers and friends. We apply it to our jobs, and our golf games. We apply it to our wealth and our health. Me, too, of course.

One way I've found to surmount "if only," smooth out its karma, and find a return route to the present, is to write about it, to try and write the whole story, being completely truthful, and leaving out no details. This is my way of completing the circle, of no longer being "separate from."

Nobody sees the results of this private scribbling, and I won't burden you with it, but here's what it's taught me:

That it's impossible to tell the whole story, which almost always involves other people. I can't know what's in someone else's mind or how they really feel, even though I used to think I did.

It's impossible to be completely truthful. It always takes more than one rewrite before the self-serving slant is pushed upright.

It's impossible to leave out no details. But in searching for them, and in finding some of them, there's a good chance of getting to higher ground, meeting my "if only" in a brighter light, and finally being "at one" with what is.

It would be a lie to suggest that Shingo and I chose off-grid life to atone for too many years of too much consumption. We chose it because we could afford it. And, certainly, because it's so beautiful here.

But as an ecological payback, it just might work. It shrinks our flat-footed city footprint, causing us to reduce, recycle and re-use quite naturally because it's in our interest to do so. ("No need to go to the dump today. There's not much garbage.")

It forces us to be aware of electrical usage: the voltmeter in the kitchen is staring at us and when we use our $12 Walmart toaster we can see that it slurps electricity. So, too, the invaluable rice cooker, which we now never use to reheat rice, steaming it on the stove instead.

Using liquid propane to heat water and run the fridge and stove puts less stress on the environment than we did in Los Angeles, where we were cooking, refrigerating, air conditioning, and heating water with electricity made from coal, petroleum, or other polluting non-renewables.

Likewise, using the sun's energy to light the house, and run the pump, and power the appliances is a lighter way to live.

121

But it would also be a lie to say we often make these comparisons, surrounded, as we are, by over-the-top green-on-green, lush would be an understatement, jungle-boogie nature. Environmental concerns require a stretch of the imagination, though in East Hawaii we're well aware of changing weather patterns: it's much sunnier, or so you think, until it rains for a month.

We watch as scientists count whales; and scale sheer cliffs to pollinate rare plants, whose previous insect pollinator is now extinct; catch the last of the Hawaiian native birds in mist nets and test them for diseases; spy on mating turtles and seals; and attach radio transmitters to the dorsal fins of dolphins, all in order to help them survive. They fence national park lands and hunt invasive sheep to protect native plants and animals, which are barely clinging to life in their disappearing habitats.

But if I were a dolphin with a beeper on my fin, or a turtle having sex with five pairs of binoculars trained on me, or a mist-netted i'iwi bird forced to give a blood sample, like it or not, I'd be shouting, "You humans are the invasive species! Even your amends are invasive."

Sometimes the best amend is to butt out. You can't leave a big fat footprint if you're stretched out in a hammock.

But if I want to butt in, there's plenty to do.

Any issue I care about can be found on the internet. Innumerable organizations can direct my energy and use my time and money to do good. At a moment's notice, I can dive right into "Us All."

And if I have a mind to tackle it, there's a crisis out there waiting. Yes, there is. Guaranteed. There always has been and there always will be.

When the Chinese invented gunpowder in the 9th century CE, the world was supposed to come to an end. Today it's global warming, species decimation, resource depletion, over-population, nuclear proliferation and a few big, bad diseases. But once the scary headlines that currently bounce the world around like a ping pong ball have been addressed, there will be a need for something new.

Maybe someday it'll be, "People on solar panels are using more than their share of the sun!"

Or: "Humans are made up of too many atoms. Fruit flies are better for the environment!"

Don't laugh. Stranger things have happened . . .

Even if I don't have the inclination for a let's-have-more-meetings-and-fix-all-the-horrible-things-that-are-terrifying-us gig, writer Kathleen Parker (no relation to Eleanoah), whose syndicated column appears in *The Hawaii Tribune-Herald*, has some useful ideas about giving back.

She says, "Giving is: Listening. Sparing time. Not interrupting. Holding that thought. Leaving the last drop. Staying home. Turning it off. Making eye contact. Picking it up. Paying attention. Waiting."

As Maezumi Roshi used to say when he approved of something, "Kind of nice, huh?"

Perhaps my piddling positive actions won't save the world, but there's a chance they'll bail me out of at least some negative karma, caused by untamed greed, rage and wrath, and amazing, arrogant, ignorance.

Right now, I think I'll go online and send $20, the price of a flock of ducks, to Heifer International. I'll mentally apply it to my Three Poisons account.

Then, with no particular amend in mind, I'm going to go and plant some carrots.

WE'RE **STILL** STILL HERE

Well, it's been five, going on six, years, and, like The Lone Ranger and Tonto, we're still around. Birthdays have gone by, marching us further over the hill, but we're more comfortable in our rainforest home, and more comfortable with each other than ever before.

Little by little, we've fixed many of the problems we ran into when we first moved here. And we're still at it. Yesterday, Shingo installed a hanging lamp over our dining table. You can see your dinner now.

But some things haven't changed.

People often ask, "Did you ever get a street address?"

No. I haven't gone to the time-consuming trouble of finding out the names and addresses of every landowner on Road Nine, and writing to ask them to suggest, or agree to, a street name. This has to be a Hawaiian word or the name of a cultural figure, which must then be vetted by The County to make sure it's not already in use elsewhere on the island. Can you blame me?

New neighbors have expressed an interest in naming the road and getting house-numbers but so far nothing's happened.

I like the "no address" scenario, anyway. It makes a better story. It confounds off-island people, but it's no hassle here. A mainland package once arrived via UPS, redirected from Hilo as follows: Lynne Farr, Middle Of Nowhere, with lengthy handwritten instructions to my door.

Driver's License? You'd think that having no address would be a problem, but the police, who issue licenses in East Hawaii, know you're not a vagrant. There's a space on their application form for your physical whereabouts, and then they ask for your mailing address, which, in our case, is General Delivery at the post office.

"How come you're still General Delivery?" people ask, "Don't you have a post office box YET?"

Uh . . . no.

It's not that we haven't been offered one. We have. More than once.

But the first time, Shingo was preparing for a show at The Contemporary Museum in Honolulu, following which we were going to Japan. The timing for changing addresses and notifying everyone, in English and Japanese, didn't work.

Next time a box came up, I simply didn't want one. It had taken a couple of years to get everyone on the same General Delivery page: companies like 20th Century Fox who send dribs and drabs of television residual money (I once got a check for 39 cents), and Ampex Corporation, in and out of bankruptcy, represented by lots of lawyers, who are supposed to send miniscule music royalties. Huge corporations, with bigger fish to fry, don't mind mislaying your change of address and keeping your 39 cents until you set them straight, if you ever do. Better to let sleeping corporations lie.

Some people, new to Puna, are unhappy without a post office box. A numbered box helps to satisfy a mainland banker or insurance man that you do live somewhere. And, with a box, you can use your key and pick up mail any time of the day or night.

Without one, you need to arrive between 11:30 a.m. when the mail's been sorted, and 3:30 p.m. when they close. You have to go in to the P.O. and stand in line to get your mail.

But I was glad to give up the box that would have had our names on it. I'd miss saying "Hi" and having little conversations with Postmistress Jeri, or Velda or Chrissie as they bundle up the mail.

And I'd miss overhearing dialogue that opens a tiny window into people's lives . . .

Like this:

"Veteran's Day – I'll be celebrating that," a man said to no one in particular.

His age suggested a Vietnam vet.

"Semper Fi," he almost whispered as he left the post office.

My heart ached for him.

"Did you ever get that big propane tank?" is another question people ask.

No, not the huge gray thing that needed miles of expensive piping to bring the gas to the house, either that or so ugly-up an area near our front entrance it would make Martha Stewart feel nauseous.

But, after Shingo's sciatica attack, and a few more months of trying to drag heavy tanks around with a hand-cart, we realized that propane delivery was something we must look into again.

And (applause, applause) there was an answer. Two 39" tall cylinders, each holding 23.5 gallons of propane, could be delivered, tucked out of sight, and replaced, when empty, by The Gas Company. Not only that, but a self-switching thingamabob (see how I know these technical terms?) could be attached between the two tanks which would keep the propane flowing and tell us when to call for more.

Galvanized pipe had to be installed to carry the LP gas from the cylinders to the water heater, and into the kitchen to the stove and fridge, but this was a relatively easy and not very expensive thing to do, since all the destinations were close by.

Shingo did have to cut a corner off his studio to make room for cylinder delivery, but that odd rounding of the studio makes it look architecturally post-modern – Martha will not require the smelling salts.

Unfortunately but typically, the price of propane increased twice, by a total of 43 cents a gallon, in the three months after we installed the new tanks.

Gas Company reps say it can and probably will go back down, though not as far down as when we started. (No kidding!)

The main thing is: Shingo won't have to carry a propane tank ever again. He's one serene off-grid individual.

If you ask me why it took us so long to get this done, I'll reply, as usual, that we didn't know any better.

We didn't realize there was any alternative to a giant eyesore of a tank, that would cost even more, and give us the home-owner heebie-jeebies.

The new set-up seems to have improved the efficiency of our gas appliances. Our big Bosch whole-house on-demand hot water heater already made a nice hot bath but now makes one hot enough to boil a lobster, just the way Shingo likes it. And the stove heats food (and burns it) faster, at a lower setting.

Wondering why, I called Gweyn Eckart at The Gas Company. With her long years of experience and installation expertise, she's the gas guru who solved our propane problems. Gweyn says the extra efficiency is not a pipedream. It's the reality of new ¾" galvanized pipe which replaced the old gas delivery system, the skinny copper tubing – "No, no. Not to code" – we'd been living with.

This brings to mind the issue of our ½" PVC water pipes, which various plumbers have said are also too small. Realizing, now, that it's just a short hop from the water catchment tank to the kitchen and bathroom, it would probably be an easy and inexpensive job to replace it with ¾" pipe, which would pep up the puny flow of water to the bathtub and shower and make my occasional unprintable comments about the builder of our house unnecessary.

Together with the new gas pipe, ¾" PVC might also make a clothes dryer and washing machine at home a possibility. To find out, we'd need a consultation with Michael MacMillan. He, who sees all and knows all, can figure out the watts and the what-nots – like where's the soapy water going to end up? – before we make any moves.

Which is making me think about the cess pool. If clothes washing water goes there, we'll have to use bio-degradable soap and bleach, no chlorine, or risk destroying the balance of power between beneficial microbes and that other stuff that's down there. I'm still faithfully putting kindly microbes down the john once a month and hoping they're doing their unappetizing job. I certainly wouldn't want anything to keep them from it.

"Do you have enough solar panels now?" people ask when they see our increased array.

Not really. I don't know if you can ever have enough.

We added four new panels in 2010 to four older ones installed five years ago, and still have the two originals which are dedicated solely (solarly?) to the water pump. But we could use more.

There's a timing issue, however, which has to do with batteries. When you add new batteries to old, the whole battery bank sinks to its lowest level of performance, or so I believe. I'm not sure if more solar panels will require more batteries and, if they do, should we hurry to add them? That's another series of questions for Michael MacMillan next time he comes.

The four panels we added do make it possible, on a sunny day, to use an electric iron instead of the cordless butane iron I bought from Lehman's Non-Electric Catalogue, which has been mostly sitting in a drawer since we got here.

That iron was just the sort of thing a know-nothing person about to move off the grid would buy: an expensive boo-boo. It's too heavy, unwieldy, more like your great-grandmother's flat-iron than a modern appliance, and lighting the butane is un-nerving.

But I just had to have it, and I'm not the only one. I know of at least one more butane iron occupying a drawer on The Big Island. I won't mention its owner's name, but if you look at the credits at the front of this book you'll notice she designed the cover.

With the extra solar panels and a sunny sky we can vacuum without the generator. But who wants to vacuum on a sunny day?

We can make rice in the rice cooker in late afternoon, using energy from the sun, and keep it warm in the pot 'til dinnertime. As days lengthen and the sun stays longer, this becomes more and more possible: zero-carbon-footprint rice!

We're even leaving the stove plugged in, which means we can light a gas flame with the tick-tick-tick electric starter, instead of searching for a lighter.

The stove also has an electric clock. But using Rich's Switch we turn off all the electricity at night, which turns the clock off, too. It has to be reset every morning or it will blip incorrect numbers at you, over and over, until you go insane.

I'm often asked, "For a solar system to work well, don't you need constant sun?"

It couldn't hurt. But if you have to shade your eyes when you look up at the sky, your solar panels are making some energy whether the sun's out or not. With a good generator you can fill in the gaps when the voltage gets too low.

At our house, on a rainy day, we almost always use the generator at night, and sometimes need it in the daytime, too, depending, naturally, on our use of electricity.

Wet clothes on the retractable outdoor clothes-line are a sure predicter of rain. We call it the "clothes-line curse." Sometimes handwashing stays in the yard for days, through sun, rain, sun, rain, and sun, until it eventually dries. It will dry, some day, and it'll smell really good.

Clear sunny weather can mean that "Kona winds" are blowing from West to East on the Big Island. Madame Pele, in her fiery moods, usually sends the voggy clouds from her glowing red caldera in Volcano National Park to the Kona side, but, once in a long while, when Kona winds prevail, we have to slam the windows shut against the sickening smell of sulphur.

On the other hand, on a Kona day, the solar panels send the voltmeter soaring.

"How often do you need to use your woodstoves?" is another FAQ.

When there's no sun, it can be cold, especially when there's snow on Mauna Kea mountain, which happens in late winter and, sometimes early spring. This year, 2011, there was flukey snow on the mountain for a couple of days in June.

When the winds are chilled by snow, we need a fire in the morning. It takes about an hour for the house to heat up. No problem. We're back in bed with the covers up to our noses.

In January through May we usually need a fire at night. After a summer hiatus, by October and November, we'll probably want a fire again. But sometimes November can fool you and act like sunny December. If so, a fire makes the house too warm.

Just wanting the pleasure of dancing flames, we might make one anyway. It's wasteful, a blazing fire with all the windows open, but the sweet perfume of burning wood strikes a deeply primitive chord.

With five-plus years of boonie experience, we can each build a fire in either of the woodstoves using one match. But only because we finally swallowed our pride and read the manufacturers' instructions.

First a big log goes in the back of the stove: the "backlog." A smaller one goes in front. Between the two go twists of paper, a blob of a product called "Fire Liter," and small branches of dry kindling. One wooden match lights the Fire Liter, and, as it burns, new larger kindling is added, always across the flame, which is now strong enough to set a medium sized log ablaze. Adjusting the air intake gets flames flaming and red hot coals glowing. More logs can then be added any time.

To send warmed air into the room, we use an EcoFan, the best off-grid investment we ever made. It sits on top of the stove, cordless of course, made of black metal with shiny brass-colored fan blades, using heat and some unknown engineering feat, to start the fan blades moving. You can tell when your fire's getting hot enough because the EcoFan begins to twirl, looking and behaving like a Martian toy.

"Who's maintaining your road these days? Who fills the potholes?" asked my friend with the butane iron.

Not us. Not any more. Newer, younger neighbors – by that I mean people under 60 – have been keeping it passable, though it's always lumpy and bumpy and probably always will be.

My friend was impressed because it's not as lumpy and bumpy as her road, with its tire-shredding volcanic lava potholes, some of which could swallow your car.

There's not much you can do about those. You can fill them with gravel but it slides right out again.

It might sound ridiculous to say we're lucky to have a muddy dirt road, but we are.

"With no TV, what do you do for news and entertainment?" is a FAQ with a tinge of panic in it. Most people can't imagine their lives without that flickering screen and the constant blather that goes with it.

For one thing, we read old-fashioned newspapers. Shingo's is *The Hawaii Hochi* from Honolulu, in English and Japanese. I like *The Hawaii Tribune-Herald*, and *The Economist*, a weekly magazine, but can't get through them fast enough. I have an *Economist* backlog, which won't work as a backlog in the fireplace: the pages are glossy, no good for burning.

There's always the internet, though my connection is so slow I can't watch anything that moves. No videos for me, no YouTube, and no instant viewing at Netflix, just old-style DVDs via snail mail.

Did you know that DVD means "Digital Versatile Disc"? Neither did I until I looked it up online.

Via digital versatile disc we've seen too many samurai films and can't count the documentaries about nature, music, or historical events. Though we often attend live theater at the University of Hawaii in Hilo, we never leave the house to see a movie.

A friend at The Fern Acres Book Group (more about them soon) told me that her husband was lying in a hammock reading my first book *Off The Grid Without A Paddle*, and laughing, when her son came into the kitchen and asked her, "What's Dad doing?"

"He's reading a book," she said.

"Wow," said her son. "I've never seen Dad read a book before!"

We do read books, each in our own language. But Shingo has never read *Off The Grid Without A Paddle* and he won't be reading this book either, unless it's suddenly available in Japanese. Only once did we get to read the same book at the same time: *The DaVinci Code.*

There are interesting bookstores on The Big Island for new and used English language books, and there's always amazing Amazon.com, where you can find the newest or the most obscure titles and buy them with the click of a cursor. For Japanese language books, Shingo usually trades with Japanese friends.

I still appreciate the Mountain View Public & School Library where I used to use the internet, and where I still borrow books and DVDs and music CDs. Even in these days of changing modes of information delivery, it's a resource the community can't do without.

One thing Shingo and I did recently to entertain ourselves was to send away for *National Geographic*'s DNA test kit. We're participating in their "Genographic Project."

Years of DNA testing all over the world indicate that the human family originated in Southern Africa. Markers in our DNA track the travels of branches of the family throughout the ages, as they moved out of Africa and evolved into all the races on Earth.

We don't have our results yet, but Shingo says the project's scientists are going to tell him his ancestors didn't budge. He says they'll say, "You're still a monkey."

No matter where we came from, and no matter where we're going, we're happy to be here now, in our green Hawaiian home, getting a kick out of off-grid senior citizenship.

"But did you ever think of leaving?" someone recently asked.

That question was easy to answer.

No. Not even for one minute.

I asked Shingo and his reply was the same.

"I want die here," he said.

I do, too. With my (rubber) boots on.

Not that there's never been a disappointment.

For example, I'd hoped our vegetable garden would be supplying all our greens and root vegetables by now. But it's not.

It probably would be, except for the chickens.

Yes, it's "chickens" plural – very plural – again.

Jack, our former rent-a-rooster has become a semi-resident. He's here for most of the day. He must have previously been the lead singer in a heavy-metal band, because, besides his rock-star presence, he has that raucous voice. It's hard to be in the middle of an important phone call, or any phone call, when he lets loose with one of his rooster show-stoppers. Happily, he doesn't start crowing until about 7:00 a.m. He must know we like to sleep in.

Betty, his #1 wife, is also back. And Yolanda, who's now a concubine, and chicks A and B, who should rightfully be re-named hens A

132

and B, are mostly here, too. They're all grown up, have formed a gang, and have been kicking and scratching and pecking the life out of my garden.

If you've ever lived with chickens you know how destructive they can be. Incessantly looking for food, they kick at dirt or moss or cinders, scratch it out of the way, and peck until they've devoured an insect or a worm. You should see the damage they leave behind. They're almost as bad as pigs.

But I outsmarted them. (Have I lived in the backwoods too long? Who brags about outsmarting a chicken?)

I found several large wire-basket drawers left over from an old storage system. Flipped upside down, they made perfect cages over my vegetables. They let the sun and rain in, but kept the wild fowls out.

Still, Jack and his hen harem kicked and scratched at every open space in the cinder-filled ditches. I had to buy more basket/drawers at Home Depot, and spray-paint them black so they look good in front of the house, adding another $158 to the costs of cinders, fertilizer, and, uh, umbrellas.

For almost a year I'd been making compost in a barrel composter, which I emptied out, intending to dry it for a few days on the ground before adding it to the garden, but, before you could say "barbecued chicken," our visitors ATE every scrap of it.

Alright, alright, I guess they're no longer visitors. I guess they long ago became *our* chickens. Not that they ever gave us any eggs.

In the morning, after crowing a couple of times, Jack appears outside the bedroom window and pecks on the glass: his way of saying "Where's breakfast?" Shingo's thrilled to get up and provide it.

All day long it's cluckety-cluck-cluck and cock-a-doodle-doo – or ko-ke-ko-ko, if you're listening in Japanese – putting our former peace and quiet in chicken parentheses.

And our lawn is now dotted with large blobs of chicken manure. Their movements are like something out of *Beethoven's Ninth*: "Da da da dung!"

I'm tolerating these animals because of the non-stop joy they give my husband. He's crazy about the chickens.

He does realize what vandals they are, and how noisy. He even thanked me, in all sincerity, for not going out and buying a gun.

But then came the final insult. Yolanda and hen A got up on my potting bench and ate the seeds and seedlings out of several starter pots.

I was not pleased.

Then I overheard Shingo talking to Jack.

"Jack," he said, "You need tell wife make egg or Lynne sooo mad you!"

Believe it or not, that afternoon I found our first egg, not in a fluffy nest, but on the hard wooden floor in the cabinet which houses the generator.

"An egg! Honey! An egg!"

All was forgiven.

Though I must say, that egg was the most expensive egg we ever ate. As are the vegetables which are finally coming to our table from the chicken tricking garden.

But, at our age, who really cares? We loved that egg! And all the eggs that followed.

By now, we're inundated with eggs. We're giving eggs away.

Those darling eggs are just one more reason why we're STILL still here.

And why we will be until our atoms rearrange.

15

AND THEN WHAT?

"And then what?" is a favorite expression of Shingo's. It's his standard comment on all the crises of this world:

"North Korea has nuclear weapons!!!"

"And then what?

"Aloha Airlines has gone out of business!!!"

"And then what?"

"Oil is $100 . . . $115 . . . $126.72 a barrel!!!

"And then what?"

Having survived war and economic disasters (some of his own making) he's less than impressed by exclamation marks. Having no TV, he's less exposed to the politics of fear.

Or perhaps, since moving to East Hawaii, his focus has narrowed.

I don't hear him being at all blasé about the small details he observes while driving down his beloved Highway 11.

In fact, he has an alertness, an awareness, an all-out nosiness that our Philipino neighbors describe as "long-neck, big-eye."

Passing homes he knows well only because he drives by them so often, he'll note:

"Oh, window open. Careful. Rain coming."

"Oh! 1950s Ford Falcon. Like new!"

"Oh! Goat outside fence!"

And there's always an "ohhh" for the ruby red bougainvillea between Mountain View and Kurtistown which has climbed a telephone pole and spread along its wires and is never cut back by phone company tree-trimmers. Shingo assumes that's because of its incredible beauty, but it just might be because of its incredible prickliness.

In other long-neck big-eye news:

Mrs. Tanimoto and Mrs. Saito and Mrs. Watanabe continue to progress into their nineties, confirmation that Shingo is mistaken when he insists that the word "great" can only be applied to a Picasso or an Einstein.

I say these women, whom we're lucky enough to know, are great: not just great in years but great in courage, great in stick-to-it-ive-ness, great in creativity, just plain great; as is the great George Indie, provider of our woodstove wood, among the many on this island who live up to the description.

George, by the way, got a new truck. It cost him $300. It does look very shiny and new compared to his earlier rusted-out wreck. Its engine doesn't cough, it has an almost unscarred truck-bed liner, and the tailgate closes without the aid of rope.

After complimenting him on his ability to put this $300 "as is" vehicle into usable shape, he grinned and said, "Yeah, now you won't be able to say bad things about my truck."

Shingo got a rocking chair, which he says he's always wanted. It's a copy of a Bentwood rocker in black enamelled steel. Its sleek contemporary lines should allow a lot of rocking without sticking Shingo with an oldster image. Though I don't think we have to worry too much about him rocking and drooling just yet. He also got an iPhone.

Leapfrogging our previous telephone technology and escaping my "watch your minutes" control, he joined neighbor Kris's family plan. She set him up at AT&T and helped him understand the phone. He hasn't looked back.

He can make all the local and long distance calls he wants, watch YouTube and news videos, access his e-mail, do it all in English or Japanese, and do it worldwide, for the same price or less than before.

A new English word has entered his vocabulary: "App."

He can listen to techno music, or Japanese enka from the 1940s. And here's the really good part: using earbuds he can keep it to himself.

He's even texting. When Kris texted him too early one morning, he texted back, "Zzzzz."

Next thing you know he'll be using Skype from his rocker.

Not to be out-toyed, I bought an ice-cream maker, the Gelato by Lello, over the internet. It's electric but only uses the wattage of two lightbulbs, so it's a perfect off-grid machine.

I can make coffee or green tea ice cream, vanilla with real vanilla bean, lilikoi sherbet, and almond gelato. For a quick treat, I'm freezing tropical fruit juices straight from the carton.

It's become our habit to enjoy these icy desserts while soaking in a hot bath in the evening, prompting Shingo to ask, "Is this Heaven or Hell? Are we died?"

Which reminds me of an old Zen story. Stop me if you've heard this one:

A man was so rich he could pay his way to Heaven and Hell, before his death, to see which he preferred.

He went to Hell first and found an endless banquet table loaded with every imaginable delicacy. People sat on both sides of the table with long chopsticks. They could reach the food but couldn't get it into their mouths because their chopsticks were too long.

Then he went to Heaven. The scene was identical – same endless banquet, same mouth-watering food, same long chopsticks. The only difference was that people were using their chopsticks to reach across the table and feed each other.

Kind of nice, huh?

I'm going to prepare a Japanese delicacy this weekend: "Nagasaki-style braised pork". KTA Supermarket in Hilo is featuring fresh pork belly, which I'm going to turn into the least healthy entree known to mankind, featuring more fat, salt, and sugar than any human being should knowingly consume.

Smothered in garlic, marinated overnight, boiled all morning, then simmered for hours in soy sauce, sugar, and sweet sake, it's so naughty-delicious you have to eat the whole thing at one sitting, lying to yourself that it won't taste good the next day.

Taste treats add much to the pleasure of living off-grid and living to a ripe old age. But if you eat too much Nagasaki braised pork, I can't guarantee the latter.

It's taken three months, but our results have finally come in from *National Geographic*'s Genographic Project.

Delving into DNA is such an emotional quest. Both of us imagined more than DNA could ever deliver.

I fantacised finding a barbarian Pict in my female genes, one of those matrilineal Northern Scots whose fighting women (and men) defeated the invading Roman legions in the 5th century CE. They're the decidedly non-Buddhist ladies with all the tattoos and the midnight blue warpaint which they refused to take off until the last of their enemies was killed or returned the favor.

Shingo was tickled by the possibility of being a direct descendant of Genghis Khan, the fearsome Mongolian warrior of the 13th century, whose empire stretched across Asia. Having held power through his descendants for hundreds of years in civilizations where harems were the norm, his genes are evident in sixteen million living Asian men.

But not in Shingo.

His predecessors apparently just plodded their way north out of Africa and finally crossed an ice bridge into Northern Japan.

My DNA made me look more like a Roman than a Pict, since my female forebears in the British Isles were constantly driven south by freezing weather and had to wait for global warming before they could go "home."

Despite our less-than-grandiose origins, a true-life adventure was certainly lived by all our distant ancestors, and yours, who followed and hunted the herds of animals which sustained their lives, as ice ages came and went, pushing them hither and thither throughout prehistory.

According to the Genographic Project, starting around 48,000 BCE, modern humans travelled from Africa via India to Australia, with other branches heading to the Middle East, up to the Caucasus, on to Asia, and also to Europe and the far North.

In a non-ice age, a small group crossed a land bridge from Siberia over the Bering Strait into what is now North America and, during further centuries, worked their way down to Mexico and points south.

From Australia, they sailed to the Pacific islands and, eventually, to Hawaii.

Here on The Big Island we all meet again.

We have many faces now, and speak many languages, the invention of which helped our ancestors to be successful by communicating ideas, making plans, and passing on knowledge. Hawaiian, Ilocano, Japanese, Tagalog, English, Chinese, Korean, Vietnamese, Chuukese, Marshallese, Yapese, Samoan, Portugese, and Spanish are among the tongues we've created as we populated the world. (At our house it's Shinglish which may or may not allow us to communicate ideas, make plans, and pass on knowledge).

As the Hawaiians have always known, DNA proves without a doubt that we're all members of the same family. So why not take off the warpaint and reach across the table with our chopsticks now?

Let's see, what else?

Japan, as you know, had a point 9 earthquake followed by a devastating tsunami and terrifying radiation spills from several nuclear electric plants.

This was not a "Then what?" event. It was a "Shikatanai, cannot be helped" act of nature, which, nonetheless, caused much anxiety here.

Shingo's family and friends were all okay, if walking up 11 flights of stairs to get to your apartment in Tokyo, where the electricity is out, is okay. Or shopping for food in markets where the shelves are almost bare, or trying to buy gasoline when there is none, is okay. And if there's anything okay about nuclear plants leaking radiation into the air and water.

But people in Japan were more stoic about the horror than we were, in the same way that a person with an illness may be better able to cope than relatives standing by, unable to help.

We lit candles for the lost, sent our meager amount of money for the refugees, and continue to check Shingo's iPhone for updates on radiation, as he prepares for a solo show in the art gallery at Volcano National Park, and another in Kyoto next year. We hope that the overwhelming destruction will be followed by leaps of life, though, hopefully, no guinea pigs the size of rhinos, and no rhinos the size of a two story house.

A certain Mr. Bin Laden temporarily drove news from Japan off the front pages as he went to claim his virgins. I wonder how his three widows feel about that.

Meanwhile:

There are still no feral pigs in our neighborhood. We only spot them in Hilo where you can sometimes watch a family dawdling up or down the tree-filled grassy median strip dividing Highway 11 as it leads into town – root, root, root.

Even without pigs digging them up, two of our five papaya trees went on tour. But three still live, and one is making flowers – fruit, fruit, fruit.

A young art historian has taken an interest in Shingo's "Mono Ha" installations and will include photos of them in a show and catalogue she's preparing for 2012 in L.A. Because of her involvement, we've discovered that 40-year-old strips of film featuring shots of Shingo in his twenties, once used in an art piece at the Tokyo National Modern Art Museum, still exist in a rusty film can at a friend's house in Tokyo. Who's going to open that can? Will the film be viewable?

Whatever happens, it's good to know that his early work hasn't been forgotten. That's putting a special smile on his face.

We put 50 crawfish into the new large pond. They're 4 inches long and look like little lobsters. It'll take at least a year for them to grow big enough to eat, but meanwhile they'll breed and make more crawfish.

Shingo, who feeds them kitchen scraps and loves to watch them come to the surface of the pond, is already becoming protective. He warns: "Don't eat crawfish A."

As for chick A who became hen A, she disappeared for several weeks. Shingo was worrying about her as he'd worried about her mother, Betty, when she went off without leaving a note.

But this morning I saw Ms. A looking very fluffy and fat, sitting at the front of the house, next to the smiling tiki where Shingo feeds the chickens.

Then I saw one tiny yellow head peep out from the center of her breast.

And then another,

I ran to get Shingo from his studio.

As we arrived, another chick popped out, and then one more.

And then Big Mama A stood up, revealing so many fuzzy yellow baby chickens we couldn't count them all. Still can't. They move so fast. The closest we can come to a number is 20.

So now we have Jack the rooster, his old flame Betty, his daughter Yolanda, his daughter A, and step-daughter B.

And twenty chicks! TWENTY!

And then what?!!!

ACKNOWLEDGEMENTS

Thanks . . .

Like *Off The Grid Without A Paddle*, *Off The Grid And Over The Hill* is a print-on-demand book. You buy it from Amazon.com or your favorite on-line bookseller and they print one. One book! Just for the person, anywhere in the world who wants it. This means there are no leftovers and you can buy one now or in a year, or whenever. It won't go "out of print." How off the grid is that?

You can also ask for it at your local bookstore. Here in East Hawaii most people find it at Basically Books in Hilo, or Volcano Garden Arts in Volcano, or Volcano Art Center Gallery in the National Park.

From Amazon.com it's not only a print book, it's an e-book to download and read on your Kindle reader, or your iPad, iPhone, PC, Mac, Blackberry or Android-based devices.

You can ask for it at the library, too.

For all this I gratefully thank CreateSpace.com, my internet publisher, without whom *Off The Grid And Over The Hill* would not be available in all its many forms.

Thanks also to Patti Millington for her colorful and humorous cover. She's the most talented person I know with a butane iron in a drawer.

Let me introduce and thank the members of The Fern Acres Book Group, who agreed to "crowd-source" the editing of this book. Each member took more than one chapter and commented on the humor or lack of it, spelling or lack of it, and punctuation at which I'm no genius. I've incorporated their helpful notes and sincerely thank each of them for their generous input: Claudia Ziroli-Coyl, Eric Coyl, Billie McDaniel, Patti Pinto, Carol Martin, Susan Love, and Robin Stetson. If you found errors in these pages it's their fault . (Just kidding.)

Gratitude must go to the neighbors and friends who allowed themselves to appear in *Off The Grid And Over The Hill*, including Mr. X who, though gone, will never be forgotten.

Thanks!

Especially let me thank Shingo Honda for being such a good sport while I reveal too much about him. He says it's all my illusion, not the real Shingo. And he's right. It's impossible to tell the whole story.

Recently he began to worry that what I write about him, since he can't read it, may be embarrassing.

"Don't say my name," he suddenly announced. "Call me 'S'. . ."

"Really?" I said. "It's kinda late, isn't it? One book is already out and this is the sequel!"

I don't think he's serious. He's pulling my leg, but in case he's not just let me say, "Shingo, you're the best, and please don't sue me."

Now here's a sad one: Rich Reha of "Rich's Switch" passed away in May, 2010. We remember and thank him for his expert help with our home-made electricity and his example of how to live so graciously.

Before closing, I have to thank Google, the most amazing research tool ever known. I asked it broad questions, from "How old is old?" to "How many virgins?" and it was always there, wizard-like, with the answers: Google, beyond worthy of the adjective "great."

Most of all I want to say thanks to you for taking your valuable time to read *Off The Grid And Over The Hill*. I hope you got a laugh or two and maybe some useful information.

Depending on your interest, there may be more stories to come.

Thanks everyone!